100 MEDITATIONS

Cherished by the Lord

By Kathryn J. Hermes, FSP

Pauline
BOOKS & MEDIA

Library of Congress Cataloging-in-Publication Data

Hermes, Kathryn.
  Cherished by the Lord : 100 meditations / Kathryn Hermes.
    p. cm.
  ISBN-13: 978-0-8198-1605-4
  ISBN-10: 0-8198-1605-1
  1. Bible--Meditations. I. Title.
  BS491.5.H46 2012
  242'.2--dc23

                            2011033631

The Scripture quotations contained herein are from the *New Revised Standard Version Bible: Catholic Edition,* copyright © 1989, 1993, Division of Christian Education of the National Council of the Churches of Christ in the United States of America. Used by permission. All rights reserved.

Scripture texts noted as NABRE in this work are taken from the *New American Bible,* revised edition © 2008, 1991, 1986, 1970 Confraternity of Christian Doctrine, Inc., Washington, D.C. All rights reserved. No part of the *New American Bible* may be reproduced or transmitted in any form or by any means, electronic or mechanical, including photocopying, recording, or by any information storage and retrieval system, without permission in writing from the copyright owner.

The author gratefully acknowledges that 69 chapters of this present book are adapted from reflections originally written for and published by *Living Faith* magazine from 2002 to 2010.

Cover design by Rosana Usselmann

Cover photo: Steven Grange

Interior photos: Stacey Grange, Steven Grange, Ann Richard Heady, FSP

Published by Pauline Books & Media, 50 Saint Pauls Avenue, Boston, MA 02130-3491
www.pauline.org

Printed in Korea

Pauline Books & Media is the publishing house of the Daughters of St. Paul, an international congregation of women religious serving the Church with the communications media.

1 2 3 4 5 6 7 8 9   17 16 15 14 13 12

Contents

PART II

I Am Doing Something New, Says the Lord

PART III

Do Not Be Afraid; I Am with You

Trust in the Lord with All Your Heart

PART V

Lord, I Will Follow You Wherever You Go

Indexes

Invitation

I am deeply grateful to know that *Cherished by the Lord: 100 Meditations* is available to you. These meditations are for anyone who desires to reconnect with the deepest meaning of life and the utter reliability of God's love for each of us. Each meditation is short but powerfully rooted in the word of God. Each is also founded on everyday life when we experience myriad feelings and profound needs that we long to have understood and satisfied. I have discovered, and trust you will too, that it is only in connection with the Lord that our deepest needs can be fulfilled and we can find peace.

The word of God is a starting point for this connection with the Lord. The Scriptures, and especially the Gospels, as the narrative of the apostles' experience of Jesus, are meant to take us deeply into a relationship with the carpenter of Nazareth. They are meant to draw us into the offer of hope God has made to the world in his Son.

Take, for example, the time the apostles were out at sea in the midst of a terrible storm. Even with Jesus asleep in the boat they feared they would drown! These men were afraid and maybe a bit angry that Jesus didn't seem to be concerned about their plight. They needed support from Jesus, assurance that things would be okay, and assistance in getting to land. Jesus woke up and gave them so much more. Jesus offered them connection with him, relationship, and intimacy. He calmed the sea—and their hearts—and in the process they learned more deeply who Jesus wanted to be for them.

If you are tossed about on the seas of life, if you are longing for assurance that you are loved by God, if you want greater connection with yourself, with others, and with God, or if you are in a tough situation, these pages offer you the same experience as those who walked with Jesus two thousand years ago. In these meditations, meet Jesus in the Scriptures, as you are right now, with whatever concerns you. Listen to him speak, watch him act, trust him with your story. Tell him what makes you happy, what makes you sad, what thrills you, what burdens you. Let him talk to you about your life. Let him show himself to you—let him reveal his longing for intimacy with you and his desire to cherish you forever.

PART I

The Lord Delights in His People

1 *An extraordinary mercy*

Sing to the LORD a new song,
> his praise in the assembly of the faithful.
Let Israel be glad in its maker,
> the people of Zion rejoice in their king.
Let them praise his name in dance,
> make music with tambourine and lyre.
For the LORD takes delight in his people,
> honors the poor with victory.

> Ps 149:1–4 (NABRE)

"For the LORD takes delight in his people. . . ."

God loves us as if we were the center of his universe! We who have died and risen with Christ, we in whom the Son abides, we for whom Jesus answered to his Father with his life and with his death—we are the object of God's delight. We are chosen by God. Jesus spent his thirty-three years of life serving our needs with his own hands, wiping up our mess with his own blood, opening our future with his own death. The life of the Word Incarnate was not a blip on the divine screen. For all eternity God will be serving us, bent at our feet in love and mercy and compassion. God makes the impossible, possible; the unbelievable, reality. What is unlovable will melt in his hands. What is ostentatious will thrill to be a cascade of lilies in a blooming field, clothed only with the brilliance of poverty. What is afraid will stand with the certainty of the resurrection. We shy away from grandeur and expectations, but we are drawn with confidence by this extraordinary mercy that will delight us eternally.

O Love! You wash my feet and tend to my vulnerability every day! Give me eyes to see you.

2 *The first offer of love still stands*

This day the LORD, your God, is commanding you to observe these statutes and ordinances. Be careful, then, to observe them with your whole heart and with your whole being. Today you have accepted the LORD's agreement: he will be your God, and you will walk in his ways, observe his statutes, commandments, and ordinances, and obey his voice. And today the LORD has accepted your agreement: you will be a people specially his own, as he promised you, you will keep all his commandments, and he will set you high in praise and renown and glory above all nations he has made, and you will be a people holy to the LORD, your God, as he promised.

Duet 26:16–19 (NABRE)

" . . . you will be a people holy to the LORD,
your God, as he promised."

The word "command" is a harsh word to our post-modern ears. We think that commands inhibit our freedom. They lead us to erroneously define freedom as a lack of restriction or the undisturbed possibility of living a self-invested, self-centered life. But the author of Deuteronomy states, instead, that freedom comes with a *covenant relationship* with God. We are free because we are delivered from what offends God. We are free because we are who we were created to be "in the beginning" (Gen 1:1), three clue words that point to the trust and openness that existed between the first man and woman and God. There is an irreversible vulnerability in God's love that was first expressed "in the beginning" and continues to offer itself over and over again through the history and prophets of Israel, through the life, death, and resurrection of Jesus, through each of our lives. God's first offer of love still stands: *I will be your God. Will you be my people?* (cf. Ezek 37:27)

Deliver me, my God, from all that offends you—every thought, way of expressing myself, behavior, affection—that I may be all you desire me to be.

3 Undeserved blessings

"For the kingdom of heaven is like a landowner who went out early in the morning to hire laborers for his vineyard. After agreeing with the laborers for the usual daily wage, he sent them into his vineyard. . . . When those hired about five o'clock came, each of them received the usual daily wage. Now when the first came, they thought they would receive more; but each of them also received the usual daily wage. And when they received it, they grumbled against the land-owner. . . . But he replied to one of them, 'Friend, I am doing you no wrong; did you not agree with me for the usual daily wage? . . . Or are you envious because I am generous?'"

Mt 20:1–2, 9–11, 13, 15

" . . . did you not agree with me for the usual daily wage?"

In your Christian life, what do you consider your "daily wage"? Someone once asked what we would do if we met Hitler in heaven. The person next to me answered immediately, "He won't be in heaven. He can't be. I've been good my whole life, he shouldn't get the same reward as I get!" We don't know if Hitler repented or not. But the point is that this person saw heaven as the "wages" she was to receive after doing good to others and keeping the Commandments. She was entitled to heaven. She had earned it. This parable strikes to the heart of being Christian in today's culture of entitlement. We are owed nothing. It is rather a privilege that we know the commandments and have experienced the joy of being and doing for others in the spirit of Christ. In this parable, the grumbling workers miss the point entirely. Their attitude is, "God *owes* me." Jesus was teaching them to realize instead, "God *loves* me." In the ecstasy of that love they need do nothing but rejoice that others are given a share in it, even if they have done little or nothing to deserve it.

Jesus, this message is hard: to rejoice when others are blessed undeservedly. Help me know that *I* have been blessed undeservedly. Change my heart!

4 Bursting with good news

Then his father Zechariah was filled with the Holy Spirit
and spoke this prophecy:
"Blessed be the Lord God of Israel,
for he has looked favorably on his people and
redeemed them.
He has raised up a mighty savior for us
in the house of his servant David. . . .
By the tender mercy of our God,
the dawn from on high will break upon us,
to give light to those who sit in darkness and in the
shadow of death,
to guide our feet into the way of peace."

Lk 1:67–69, 78–79

"Blessed be the Lord God of Israel. . . ."

The first two chapters of Luke are filled with prophecy and announcement. Mary visits her cousin
Elizabeth and greets her, bursting with God's good news
for herself and for the world. Zechariah, his tongue
loosed by his ultimate obedience, blesses the Lord who

has visited his people to set them free and chosen Zechariah's son to prepare the way for our salvation. The angels announce the birth of the Savior, calling the littlest and most unimportant people, the shepherds, to come in awe and wonder to see for themselves. There is a lot of scurrying about, a lot of tidings of great joy, a lot of celebration. Sounds like Christmas! Zechariah, Mary, the angels, and the shepherds not only teach us how to celebrate Christmas, but how to live as Christian disciples. We have good news for our families and for our world. We need a disciplined retraining of our thoughts and desires until we, too, are bursting with joy over this good news from God. As Christians we are ennobled, lifted up, glorified, divinized because of what Zechariah proclaims: God has set the power of salvation in the center of our lives. Nothing is more wonderful than this God who has come to be with us.

Lord, I get so lost in the labyrinth of my thoughts—in patterns of competition, self-importance, and cynicism. May the dawn from on high bring lightness to my step and your joy to my life.

5 A new name

Then Abram fell on his face; and God said to him, "As for me, this is my covenant with you: You shall be the ancestor of a multitude of nations. No longer shall your name be Abram, but your name shall be Abraham; for I have made you the ancestor of a multitude of nations. I will make you exceedingly fruitful; and I will make nations of you, and kings shall come from you. I will establish my covenant between me and you, and your offspring after you throughout their generations, for an everlasting covenant, to be God to you and to your offspring after you."

Gen 17:3–7

"I will establish my covenant between me and you,
and your offspring after you. . . ."

I remember riding a bus last year. As I took in the ads, storefronts, billboards, and people carrying bags boasting logos and internet addresses in large letters, I suddenly felt as though everything around me was screaming: "Buy me! Buy me! Buy me!" I felt like my identity had been reduced to being a faceless consumer as various companies vied for my money-spending power. In that moment I experienced the dehumanizing reality of persons reduced to victims in a global market, where the best price and the most power wins. God's words to Abraham, however, point out to us that we are more than our spending power. We are persons who are in covenant with God. In this covenant we discover what it is to be *truly* human: sought out by God, loved, embraced, committed to by the One who was, who is, and who ever will be. This covenant assures us post-moderns that the identity we so desperately seek is found, not in designer clothes and plush waterfront homes, but in the arms of a loving God who can't abandon us.

My Lord, I hunger so much to know my life has meaning. Is it too much to ask you to call *me* by a new name? Tell me who you've created me to be. . . .

6 Keep your eyes open

Let love be genuine; hate what is evil, hold fast to what is good; love one another with mutual affection; outdo one another in showing honor. Do not lag in zeal, be ardent in spirit, serve the Lord. Rejoice in hope, be patient in suffering, persevere in prayer.

Rom 12:9–12

" . . . be ardent in spirit. . . ."

In autumn, the colorful array of changing leaves outside my office window turns into winter's barren bleakness, symbolic of what often happens to our spirits. We live a spiritual rhythm of ups and downs, fullness and barrenness, blossom and decay. The downs pave the way for the ups; barrenness creates the possibility of refilling; times of decay fertilize the new blossoms in our lives. When St. Paul says, "Be ardent in spirit," he is no doubt referring to this ongoing cycle of life and death, but I believe he is thinking of something more. I often open books at random and spot read. A few months ago I came across this definition of prayer in *Teresa of Ávila—God Alone Suffices*: "To pray is to think of Jesus while loving him." It was as if a match had been struck within me. Those simple words ignited my brittle spirit into an ardent fire that burned away bad habits and replaced them with a yearning for holiness. It is the Holy Spirit who ignites these spiritual fires within us that make us long for more. Paul knew this, because the Spirit had transformed his ways of thinking, acting, and loving, making him a new creature in Christ. So keep your eyes open. The Spirit will use something in your everyday experience to ignite your spirit and inflame your heart.

Holy Spirit, stir up the ashes of my life and relight my inner fire. Amen.

7 *Wordlessly embrace his feet*

After the Sabbath, as the first day of the week was dawning, Mary Magdalene and the other Mary came to see the tomb . . . the angel said . . . "Then go quickly and tell his disciples, 'He has been raised from the dead, and he is going before you to Galilee; there you will see him. . . .'" Then they went away quickly from the tomb, fearful yet overjoyed, and ran to announce this to his disciples. And behold, Jesus met them on their way and greeted them. They approached, embraced his feet, and did him homage. Then Jesus said to them, "Do not be afraid. Go tell my brothers to go to Galilee, and there they will see me."

Mt 28:1, 5, 7–10 (NABRE)

"And behold, Jesus met them on their way and greeted them. They approached, embraced his feet, and did him homage."

The image of prayer found in this Gospel passage speaks to me in a particular way. The women, fresh from seeking among the dead the One whom they loved, bump into the Lord who was deliberately crossing their path. Jesus's death had shattered the world of his first followers. I can imagine the news of the crucifixion passing quickly from one disciple to another: the hushed suspense, the quiet agony, the shock, the fear, the sorrow. Then suddenly, less than three days later, they literally run into him, alive. Jesus must have stood there with exquisite tenderness, his heart full of compassion for their sorrow. I wonder if they stopped to notice the kindness in his eyes, for they were already bowed in adoration, blessing the ground upon which their Lord walked. When I find it difficult to pray, I join the women on the morning of the resurrection, and from the roots of my being, I adore. Wordlessly, I embrace his feet. Or I stop to notice the way Jesus looks at me, what his eyes say. If that is all we do when we pray, it is enough.

You are alive! You are here! You are my life's path! You are the way! You meet me every day! Jesus, Risen One, I adore you.

8 *God saves what he has made*

But you, O LORD, are enthroned forever;
>   your name endures to all generations.
You will rise up and have compassion on Zion,
>   for it is time to favor it;
>   the appointed time has come. . . .
The nations will fear the name of the LORD,
>   and all the kings of the earth your glory.
For the LORD will build up Zion;
>   he will appear in his glory.
He will regard the prayer of the destitute,
>   and will not despise their prayer.

Ps 102:12–13, 15–17

"For the LORD will build up Zion; he will appear in his glory.
>   *He will regard the prayer of the destitute,*
>   *and will not despise their prayer."*

God reaches out to the people who are his beloved. Through the prophets, God tells them that their choice to love and follow other gods is a serious offense to their relationship with him. Now an incurable wound, an injury past healing, stands between them and God.

Nevertheless, God promises to restore the relationship. *Look at this*, God says, *I shall restore you. When you return to your land there will be thanksgiving. Songs of joy will replace your tears, and happiness will fill your houses.* God manifests his glory to his people by saving them, by restoring the relationship they have chosen to sever by disowning him. God manifests himself as the supreme sovereign, as the king of glory. But God's sovereignty is not characterized by a ruthless power, a selfish subjugation of everyone and everything to his own desires and ambitions. God is above our petty power plays and greater than our rejection of his love. God is love. God cannot be nor do anything except love. The whole universe is full of his mighty deeds. He manifests the splendor of his majesty by reaching out and saving what he has made, transfiguring and transforming us into images of his Son so that we too might one day participate in his glory for all eternity.

Transfigure and transform me in you, Jesus. Fill me with the radiance of God. Amen.

9 *Love extravagantly*

Six days before the Passover Jesus came to Bethany, the home of Lazarus, whom he had raised from the dead. There they gave a dinner for him. Martha served, and Lazarus was one of those at the table with him. Mary took a pound of costly perfume made of pure nard, anointed Jesus' feet, and wiped them with her hair. The house was filled with the fragrance of the perfume.

Jn 12:1–3

"Martha served. . . ."

I have just finished a whirlwind project under a tight deadline. In this type of situation I almost always end up, to my embarrassment, talking too hastily, exaggerating, and pontificating. The project sucks me out of the space inside my spirit where I offer quiet hospitality to Jesus. I look everywhere else except into the Lord's quiet eyes. In this Gospel, there is silence within Lazarus's home. Lazarus and his two sisters are welcoming Jesus, paying attention to him, serving him. Not a word is said by any of them. In fact, Jesus defends the extravagance of their love for him. The others in the scene speak harsh and violent words—they are people who have taken their eyes off Jesus and have started looking in the other directions of their hearts' distorted desires.

Jesus, keep my eyes on you. Even in the whirlwind of daily activities help me grab onto you more tightly, serving you and pouring out the oil of my love for you in your Church.

10 *Our deepest longings*

Long ago God spoke to our ancestors in many and various ways by the prophets, but in these last days he has spoken to us by a Son, whom he appointed heir of all things, through whom he also created the worlds. He is the reflection of God's glory and the exact imprint of God's very being, and he sustains all things by his powerful word. When he had made purification for sins, he sat down at the right hand of the Majesty on high, having become as much superior to angels as the name he has inherited is more excellent than theirs.

Heb 1:1–4

" . . . he has spoken to us by a Son. . . ."

In this passage from Hebrews, Christ, whom angels glorified, shepherds adored, and kings honored, is presented to us. Who is this Christ? What does he mean for me? This Christ, this Son of God, is the answer to our deepest longings to know that we are loved, that our lives have meaning, that we have a future and that it is good. From the quiet Galilean hills explodes a hope, a promise, a guarantee. Christ has been weighed down with our sins, our pains, our illnesses, and our tears. He has borne them all. He has died and all this has died with him. Christ has risen, and we too rise with him. He has conquered evil and death. We see our future in his triumph over death and in his ascension to the Father's right hand. In him we are taken into the circle of life and love within the Trinity. We are held and embraced there, hidden and protected. Such awe! God "has spoken to us. . . . When [his Son] had made purification for sins, he sat down at the right hand of the Majesty on high." He lives and so *we* will live forever.

Jesus, you live and so I will live! Forever! Amen.

11 *His gracious act of redemption*

O LORD, my heart is not lifted up,
   my eyes are not raised too high;
I do not occupy myself with things
   too great and too marvelous for me.
Bu I have calmed and quieted my soul,
   like a weaned child with its mother;
   my soul is like the weaned child that is with me.
O Israel, hope in the LORD
   from this time on and forevermore.

Ps 131

" . . . I have calmed and quieted my soul. . . ."

God wants us to be content, as content as a baby in its mother's arms. I don't know about you, but there is a lot about life today that makes this seem like a pipe dream. A contented child in its mother's arms experiences safety. Contentment also means being completely satisfied, with no need to look for anything else. A contented baby isn't reaching out for diversion or entertainment. A quiet child isn't squirming to get out of its mother's arms to go running off down the street. As adults, however, contentment doesn't come so easily. We no longer experience personal, financial, or even national security. Each new release of a digital gadget restarts the itch of dissatisfaction till we have made the decision whether or not to purchase it. Many of us don't particularly like the role that is ours in the world: it might be too small, too tight, too hectic, too heavy. We cast around for something else that seems like a better fit. Psalm 131 offers us a secret for contentment: look to God and not to yourself. See what God has done in his gracious and marvelous act of redemption. Renounce any source of significance or security other than God.

O God, I have calmed and quieted my soul, content with all you give me, asleep in your care for me.

12 *How could we fear?*

I will make a covenant of peace with them; it shall be an everlasting covenant with them; and I will bless them and multiply them, and will set my sanctuary among them forevermore. My dwelling place shall be with them; and I will be their God, and they shall be my people. Then the nations shall know that I the LORD sanctify Israel, when my sanctuary is among them forevermore.

Ezek 37:26–28

> *"I will make a covenant of peace with them;*
> *it shall be an everlasting covenant with them. . . ."*

This passage, with its mounting joy and jubilant hope for an eternal covenant, is set in juxtaposition to the seeming darkness and threat of death in the final chapters of the Gospels, which recount the establishment of the New Covenant. What went wrong? Or perhaps we should ask what went right, that this covenant promised through the centuries should be written in the blood of the Son of God? The passion and death of Jesus makes visible to us the extent to which God goes to establish this covenant that sets us free to love him and to live entirely for him. God poured out all his love for us when he sent his Son to become one of us. The Son poured out all his love for us when he remained as vulnerable and obedient as a "lamb that is led to the slaughter" (Isa 53:7) and experienced with us and for us our greatest enemy: death. Since Pentecost the Holy Spirit has been poured out in love on us, as a promise and guarantee that this covenant can never be broken. Humanity was unable to keep its part of the eternal covenant. So God himself, in Jesus, has kept our side of the covenant for us. What a love. *What a love!* God himself did what we could not do ourselves. Could there be anything to fear from such a love?

Such a love! Jesus, I trust in you!

13 We're beloved, desired, died for

"To the LORD our God belongs justice; to us, people of Judah and inhabitants of Jerusalem, to be shamefaced, as on this day—to us, our kings, rulers, priests, and prophets, and our ancestors. We have sinned in the LORD's sight and disobeyed him. We have not listened to the voice of the LORD, our God, so as to follow the precepts the LORD set before us. From the day the LORD led our ancestors out of the land of Egypt until the present day, we have been disobedient to the LORD, our God, and neglected to listen to his voice."

Bar 1:15–19 (NABRE)

". . . to us . . . to be shamefaced, as on this day. . . ."

In the interest of a healthy self-esteem, this passage may cause some nervous shifting in the pews. *Why do these uncomfortable readings keep showing up? Let's hear again the story of the lilies of the field.* Indeed, taken in isolation, this passage on the justice of God can seem overly harsh. No passage of Scripture, however, can be separated from the whole. It has been said that if the Song of

Songs were the only book of Scripture, we would have all we need to understand God and salvation history. The conjugal imagery of the lover's desire for the beloved in this short, unpretentious book of love-poems, unlocks the meaning of the rest of the Bible, and of this passage in particular. Why are we "shamefaced"? Why does Jesus mourn over us as he did over the cities that had witnessed his miracles and power? Because we have been *beloved*, courted, desired, died for. We have ostentatiously held on to pennies when God was ready to make us millionaires. The impassioned divine Lover would have us be the darling of his heart. This passage is not an angry invective. These are the words of broken hearts—both human and divine—hearts that desire love, hearts that will not rest until they are loved and have proven their love to each other.

What can I do to prove my love for you, O everlasting Love!

14 *Jesus chooses you and me*

He went up the mountain and called to him those whom he wanted, and they came to him. And he appointed twelve, whom he also named apostles, to be with him, and to be sent out to proclaim the message, and to have authority to cast out demons. So he appointed the twelve: Simon (to whom he gave the name Peter); James son of Zebedee and John the brother of James (to whom he gave the name Boanerges, that is, Sons of Thunder); and Andrew, and Philip, and Bartholomew, and Matthew, and Thomas, and James son of Alphaeus, and Thaddaeus, and Simon the Cananaean, and Judas Iscariot, who betrayed him.

Mk 3:13–19

"So he appointed the twelve. . . ."

Imagine a father looking for a lost child. He wants help, so he puts together a search party. However, instead of calling on the FBI, police, and detectives, the father chooses a gang member, a child, a homeless person who knows all the streets in town, a mother from the neighborhood, a thief, and a murderer just released from prison. This would certainly make the evening news! In fact, people would probably scoff: "He's crazy! He's ruining his chance of saving his child!" Others would claim these people couldn't be trusted to love his child the way the father does. Actually, a couple of these characters might turn out to be the heartbroken father's worst nightmare. This, however, is precisely what happened when Jesus appointed twelve uneducated, unprepared, and unlikely men to help him in the very delicate work of saving the human race. They themselves were part of the humanity that needed salvation. If Jesus wanted the job done right, why didn't he choose angels he could trust? What mystery that he entrusted himself instead to family, friends, disciples, and women "who provided for" him (Lk 8:3). Today he entrusts himself to you and me.

Never, Lord, will I complain about others in the Church now that I see how you have trusted us from the beginning to carry out your Father's plan for salvation. Nothing we can do can destroy the power of that plan. Thy Kingdom come!

15 *By grace we are saved*

But God, who is rich in mercy, out of the great love with which he loved us even when we were dead through our trespasses, made us alive together with Christ—by grace you have been saved—and raised us up with him and seated us with him in the heavenly places in Christ Jesus, so that in the ages to come he might show the immeasurable riches of his grace in kindness toward us in Christ Jesus. For by grace you have been saved through faith, and this is not your own doing; it is the gift of God. . . . For we are what he has made us, created in Christ Jesus for good works, which God prepared beforehand to be our way of life.

Eph 2:4–8, 10

"For we are what he has made us,
created . . . for good works. . . ."

This is a serious consideration. God has already destined certain works to be an important part of the Christian life. How do we discover what they are? There are so many good things we could do; how do we know which specific deeds God desires most of us? This passage from the Letter to the Ephesians is full of clues. Words such as "rich in faithful love," "through the great love with which he loved us," and "it is through grace that you have been saved" tip us off. God has planned a tremendous work of art for humanity and civilization. This artistic creation is a direct reflection of God's love and life. It is that simple. The Father, from all eternity, loved the Son. The Son turned around and, instead of holding on to this love which he had received, gave it away. He emptied himself, became a man, walked among us, lived our life, and died our death, so that, as the Father had done, he could pour himself out in love for us who needed salvation. It is by grace that we are saved. The deeds God desires of us are self-emptying acts of service of others, love to the point of giving our lives for one another.

Jesus, make my life a work of art. May I love others with a faithful love that seeks their good before my own.

16 *An ongoing conversation*

O that you would tear open the heavens and come down,
   so that the mountains would quake at your
      presence. . . .
When you did awesome deeds that we did not expect,
   you came down, the mountains quaked at your
      presence. . . .
Yet, O LORD, you are our Father;
   we are the clay, and you are our potter;
   we are all the work of your hand.

Isa 64:1, 3, 8

" . . . we are the clay, and you are our potter. . . ."

One of my favorite images of God is that of a gardener, or a potter. When I plant, not being a gardener myself, I dig a hole in the dirt and put the plant in its new home. The end. I don't weed, landscape, care for it, or water it. Once, my mother took us kids to a ceramics class. It was okay, but as soon as we had finished, my interest dropped. I wasn't invested in creating things. God, however, as gardener or potter, is deeply invested in what he creates. The image of potter is often portrayed as an image of power: God chooses how to shape the clay. For me the image of potter is intimately one with the image of God pouring himself into his creation. It is an image of love. I can hear God listening closely to everything we say as he shapes our lives. The shaping of the vessel is part of an ongoing conversation of love between potter and clay. On a particularly busy day, I (the clay) may tell God (the potter) that I am tired. I need help. It is characteristic of God to bend over the little vessel he is loving into being and care for me.

Listen closely, God, to the whisper of my heart. Bend over your creature, here, and let me know your ever tender love.

17 *Held as a child*

Bless the LORD, O my soul,
>   and all that is within me,
>   bless his holy name.

Bless the LORD, O my soul,
>   and do not forget all his benefits—

who forgives all your iniquity,
>   who heals all your diseases,

who redeems your life from the Pit,
>   who crowns you with steadfast love and mercy,

who satisfies you with good as long as you live
>   so that your youth is renewed like the eagle's.

>   . . . the LORD has compassion for those who fear him.

For he knows how we were made;
>   he remembers that we are dust.

Ps 103:1–5, 13b–14

" . . . *who crowns you with steadfast love and mercy.* . . ."

I have a friend whose heart was broken in a failed relationship. He had trusted. He had hoped. He had
loved. He had dreamed. And in the end his love had been
betrayed. I watched with wonder and compassion as he

suffered and, in the pain, was transformed. Psalm 103 unfolded before me in the path he took during the years that followed his separation and divorce. He struggled with his own contribution to the failed relationship. However, God wasn't interested in that. God delights in us too much to let our relationship with him get stuck in fault-finding. Those who open their hearts to God in these pained life situations find their youth renewed much like the eagle who molts. The first lines of Psalm 103 outline a transformative process: iniquity is forgiven; disease is healed; God's love and mercy crowns us, satisfies us, and renews us like the eagle.

God, you know we are dust and unable to struggle through life's issues alone. Hold us as a child, nourished and secure in its mother's womb, renewing us over and over again, giving us new life and a new future. Amen.

18 *Creative generosity*

Then I saw a new heaven and a new earth; for the first heaven and the first earth had passed away, and the sea was no more. . . . And I heard a loud voice from the throne saying,

"See, the home of God is among mortals.
He will dwell with them;
they will be his peoples,
and God himself will be with them;
he will wipe every tear from their eyes.
Death will be no more;
mourning and crying and pain will be no more,
for the first things have passed away."

And the one who was seated on the throne said, "See, I am making all things new."

Rev 21:1, 3–5

"See, I am making all things new."

God has intervened in human history. First, he cre-ated us. Then he called the patriarch Abraham, the father of the Chosen People. He rescued his people from

Egypt through Moses. In David, he provided for his people a king after his own heart. He himself came and lived among us in Jesus, Son of Mary and Son of God. Through his death, resurrection, and ascension, Jesus reconciled us with his Father. He is now seated at God's right hand, where we will also be one day. Just as an adult loves to surprise a child with a new gift or opportunity, God's delight is to do something new for us. Have you experienced anything unexpected from God lately? If we reflect on all the ways God has come to live in our neighborhood, mysteries which we celebrate annually in the liturgical feasts of Christmas, Holy Thursday, Good Friday, and Easter, we know that something new and unexpected has been given to us. *We* are that newness. We have been given a new identity by God's interrupting human history with his love. For all eternity, we will be inundated with wave upon wave of the creative generosity of God toward us.

Interrupt my life, Father, Son, and Spirit, and do something new!

19 Broken open with glory

In the beginning when God created the heavens and the earth, the earth was a formless void and darkness covered the face of the deep, while a wind from God swept over the face of the waters.

Then God said, "Let there be light"; and there was light.

. . . Then God said, "Let us make humankind in our image, according to our likeness; and let them have dominion over the fish of the sea, and over the birds of the air, and over the cattle, and over all the wild animals of the earth, and over every creeping thing that creeps upon the earth."

So God created humankind in his image, in the image of God he created them; male and female he created them.

Gen 1:1–3, 26–27

"So God created. . . ."

When God created us he took a risk, a big risk. He created us free. He gave us quite a bit of latitude. He let us experience a wonderful relationship with him, as he walked with Adam and Eve in the cool of the garden. God wooed us with his presence that we might choose his love, and in that choice, choose what was best for ourselves. Anyone who has trusted another—friend, spouse, or child—only to have that trust betrayed knows a tiny bit of what God was all about. From the beginning, then, God's position toward his creatures was one of infinite vulnerability and freedom. It had to be this way because this is characteristic of the way the Persons of the Trinity relate to one another. If they wanted us one day to live within that eternal dance of Trinitarian love, we needed to learn from the very beginning how to truly live and love. Jesus had to come to show us how to live in vulnerability and love. From his birth to his death he refused the way of power. Just as he, in the end, was resurrected and given glory at the Father's right hand, we too, in walking the way of love, will find our lives broken open with glory when we least expect it.

Break open my life, O Holy Trinity, in glory this day.

20 God's treasured possession!

For you are a people holy to the LORD your God; the LORD your God has chosen you out of all the peoples on earth to be his people, his treasured possession.

It was not because you were more numerous than any other people that the LORD set his heart on you and chose you—for you were the fewest of all peoples. It was because the LORD loved you and kept the oath that he swore to your ancestors. . . . Know therefore that the LORD your God is God, the faithful God who maintains covenant loyalty with those who love him and keep his commandments, to a thousand generations. . . .

Deut 7:6–9

" . . . the faithful God . . . maintains covenant loyalty. . . ."

My brother is a police officer. One day he alerted me to a video, posted online, of college students being interviewed during a campus riot at a university in the town where he serves. The prevailing attitude of the interviewees was: "How dare the police stop our fun!

What have the police ever done for you or me anyway?" We can be horrified at their attitude, but if we look closely, many adults have the same attitude on a larger scale: *Why do we have to follow the Ten Commandments? Why can't we do what we want and live the way we want?* Good question. Why do we have to obey God anyway? We are God's treasured possession, his people, holy to him, chosen, loved. God has been faithful to us throughout all of human history and will show this fidelity for all eternity. It is because we are God's people that we obey him. Submission expresses our recognition of our place in this special relationship as well as our trust that God always intends our well-being. I can understand how some college students may not yet be at the point of taking the long view of life. But you and I? We live in the mystery of salvation history.

What wonder to be a child of God, a brother or sister of Jesus the Christ, a temple of the Holy Spirit!

PART II

I Am Doing Something New, Says the Lord

21 *An immense love*

For I am about to create new heavens
　　and a new earth;
the former things shall not be remembered
　　or come to mind.
But be glad and rejoice for ever
　　in what I am creating;
for I am about to create Jerusalem as a joy,
　　and its people as a delight.
I will rejoice in Jerusalem,
　　and delight in my people;
no more shall the sound of weeping be heard in it,
　　or the cry of distress.

Isa 65:17–19

"For I am about to create new heavens and a new earth. . . ."

In this passage, we are forced to stop and face the over-whelmingly magnificent message of redemption: God is doing something new! It's not that God realized he had made a mistake at first. It's not that we had botched things up so badly that God decided to scrap everything and begin again with new people. Isaiah instead is painting a vision of love that has grown so immense that it can create life, hope, and a future even in the midst of mistakes, sin, and death. This compassion is so divine that it straightens bent limbs, raises dead bodies and spirits, and transforms the dull and callous of heart. God will stop at nothing to make right our erring ways. He doesn't need to start over. Yesterday I saw a brave flower poking its way up through a crack in the sidewalk. The divine Lover is like this. Nothing can get in his way. He is unstoppable, for he has it in mind to create something new of your life and mine.

Yes, Lord! Don't stop! Don't let me block your way! Do all that you desire to accomplish in my life!

22 *Sought out by God*

For in him all the fullness of God was pleased to dwell, and through him God was pleased to reconcile to himself all things, whether on earth or in heaven, by making peace through the blood of his cross. And you who were once estranged and hostile in mind, doing evil deeds, he has now reconciled in his fleshly body through death, so as to present you holy and blameless and irreproachable before him—provided that you continue securely established and steadfast in the faith, without shifting from the hope promised by the gospel that you heard, which has been proclaimed to every creature under heaven.

Col 1:19–23

"And you . . . he has now reconciled. . . ."

The other night I realized something about myself: I tend to make everything a project, and, true to form, I make my relationship with God a project too. It may seem to be a good thing to be intent on growing in relationship with God. And it is true that my growing friendship with God hinges in part on the interest, love, and presence God and I show each other. But I often forget that Jesus himself *has accomplished* something that has created my "status" in this relationship. Before we were even born, humanity was reconciled to God, and through Baptism you and I got the full package deal. We are members of the family—premium membership, paid in full, the whole nine yards. We are children of God, and Jesus is bound and determined to present us to his Father holy and irreproachable at the end. St. Paul knew this—for God had sought him out and dramatically changed the direction of his life. This life-changing God whom Paul preaches is our hope and our salvation!

Lord, when I'm sure that the tangled confusion of my life is irredeemable, remind me of my place in your family.

23 Washed clean

Wash yourselves; make yourselves clean;
    remove the evil of your doings
    from before my eyes;
cease to do evil,
    learn to do good;
seek justice,
    rescue the oppressed,
defend the orphan,
    plead for the widow.
Come now, let us argue it out,
    says the LORD:
though your sins are like scarlet,
    they shall be like snow;
though they are red like crimson,
    they shall become like wool.

Isa 1:16–18

" . . . though your sins are like scarlet, they shall be like snow. . . ."

I have met many who have difficulty with confession.
I too struggled with the sacrament of Reconciliation
for years. The regular rotation of saying the same thing,

hearing the same thing, and reciting the same penance seemed like a divine laundry service for my soul, rather than an intimate encounter with Jesus that gradually intensified my union with him. This Scripture passage uses words such as learn, seek, and plead to convey a sense of progressive growth that should be a part of this sacrament. These words have helped me make my peace with confession. In preparation, I ask Jesus, *What in my life most jeopardizes our relationship?* I never get the same answer. It is always an unexpected and often uncomfortable revelation of a part of my life God wants to heal. I begin my confession with this discovery and by describing what God has been doing recently in my life. It is God's revelation and activity that help me bring into the light areas of my life that he wants to make white as snow.

Lord, I hear the eagerness of your heart to wipe away my sins, to transform me more completely into your disciple. I join my eagerness to yours. Lead me into a more mature celebration of Reconciliation that I may live ever more passionately as your disciple.

24 Intimacy

When it was evening, he took his place with the twelve; and while they were eating, he said, "Truly I tell you, one of you will betray me." And they became greatly distressed and began to say to him one after another, "Surely not I, Lord?" He answered, "The one who has dipped his hand into the bowl with me will betray me. The Son of Man goes as it is written of him, but woe to that one by whom the Son of Man is betrayed! It would have been better for that one not to have been born." Judas, who betrayed him, said, "Surely not I, Rabbi?" He replied, "You have said so."

Mt 26:20–25

" . . . the one who has dipped his hand into the bowl with me. . . ."

How close Judas was to Jesus—within an arm's reach. Surely, if he asked Jesus the question, *It is not I, Lord, is it?* he would have had to look directly into the Savior's eyes. Usually such intimacy produces trust and love. Although Judas held a particular place in the history of salvation, in a certain sense he represents all of humanity who has ever rejected complete and trustful obedience to God and looked out for our own best interests, afraid to look directly into our God's eyes. We too are close enough to Jesus to share his table. We eat his Body and drink his Blood. But when we look in those eyes we know something Judas did not know at that Pasch. Even if we betray our Lord and Savior, even if we sell him for "thirty pieces of silver" (Mt 26:15), those eyes of love will never stop looking into our hearts. That is the mysterious and mind-blowing reality that humanity learned only after the death and resurrection of Jesus. The betrayal of our sin brings about the absolute proof of infinite compassion. God is mightier than our puny efforts at independence and our foolish attempts at power. So let us dip our hand into the dish with Jesus, that the closeness and the intimacy might melt away our selfish desires once and for all.

My Lord, remind me that I am ever within an arm's reach of infinite compassion and forgiveness.

25 *A humble love*

"While I was on my way and approaching Damascus, about noon a great light from heaven suddenly shone about me. I fell to the ground and heard a voice saying to me, 'Saul, Saul, why are you persecuting me?' I answered, 'Who are you, Lord?' Then he said to me, 'I am Jesus of Nazareth whom you are persecuting.' Now those who were with me saw the light but did not hear the voice of the one who was speaking to me. I asked, 'What am I to do, Lord?' The Lord said to me, 'Get up and go to Damascus; there you will be told everything that has been assigned to you to do.'"

Acts 22:6–10

"Get up and go to Damascus; there you will be told everything that has been assigned to you to do."

All of St. Paul's teaching to his beloved Christian communities flows from this first hard lesson he learned from Jesus the Master: great ideas—no matter how much you can justify them or how righteous you think you are—are dangerous when they are pursued apart from dependence on God and humble membership in community. Paul was not a bad man. He thought he had things figured out: the Christians were too much of a threat with their crazy ideas about this dead man they claimed had risen. Jesus, however, showed himself to Paul as very much alive and intimately connected to a human community. Paul had to teach this lesson over and over to the first Christian communities, and we find it difficult to learn as well. All too often we are intransigent in our way of dealing with one another and assessing one another's viewpoints. People who claim they are better than others, more intelligent than others, more right than others, more righteous than others, have yet to learn the lesson of Pauline conversion: dependent faith and humble love, as we together are built up into community.

Paul, stopped in your tracks by the Lord, obtain for us a true conversion. May we too begin to truly know the joyful message of the Christian Gospel and be the Lord's witnesses to all the world.

26 Restored relationships

> Do not judge, and you will not be judged; do not condemn, and you will not be condemned. Forgive, and you will be forgiven; give, and it will be given to you. A good measure, pressed down, shaken together, running over, will be put into your lap; for the measure you give will be the measure you get back.
>
> Lk 6:37–38

"Do not judge, and you will not be judged. . . ."

Though I desire God to show me mercy, generosity, understanding, and forgiveness, I have to admit I sometimes have a hard time extending this same liberality toward others. Why is this so? Our judgments proceed from our beliefs. Beliefs can be a simple desire: "a good family eats together"; an erroneous idea: "Christians don't get angry"; a dangerous attitude: "people should not oppose me"; or a lifestyle choice: "a successful standard of living means we have two cars." Based on our beliefs we weigh others' behavior. Unless they are transformed by the Gospel, our beliefs lead to judgments that create disunity and pain. *Biblical judgment*, however, is not aimed at punishment but at restoring relationship. Here precisely is the rub. It is more satisfying and much easier to harshly condemn others from the perspective of unexamined beliefs. Every line in this Gospel selection, instead, is about relationship. We are called to analyze our beliefs, weigh them according to the criteria of the Gospel, correct some (probably many) of them, and focus on restoring relationships. Happiness flows from overcoming the human propensity to condemn others, and instead working generously to build up relationships with them.

Generous forgiveness and infinite mercy of God, flow through me into the lives of all.

27 Treat me with love

Who is a God like you, pardoning iniquity
    and passing over the transgression
    of the remnant of your possession?
He does not retain his anger forever,
    because he delights in showing clemency.
He will again have compassion upon us;
    he will tread our iniquities under foot.
You will cast all our sins
    into the depths of the sea.

Mic 7:18–19

"You will cast all our sins into the depths of the sea."

This is an interesting image, one that is perhaps a bit misleading. It could give us the idea that our sins are objects distinct from us. By casting them into the sea we could conclude that they have no real impact on us or on our relationship with God. But from the Garden of Eden, to the Chosen People's rebellion against the Lord, to the Prodigal Son who takes his life into his own hands and turns his back on the Father, to the hill of Calvary, it is clear that how we deal with sin is deeply connected with who we become. In these biblical passages, sin is defined as a distorted desire to *break free* from divine prohibition, as a cynical belief that God's demands are *contrary* to our interests. Sound familiar? Any parent should recognize the characteristics of children who want to break away from their parent's authority. As spiritual children, we at times also choose this so-called freedom rather than acknowledge the Love that sustains our lives.

Lord, show me how short-sighted, self-interested, and self-indulgent I still am in parts of my life. Open my eyes to your true identity: Love, you who can only treat me with Love, and desire that I live wholly in Love.

28 *Catch my attention*

In the beginning was the Word, and the Word was with God, and the Word was God. He was in the beginning with God. All things came into being through him, and without him not one thing came into being. What has come into being in him was life, and the life was the light of all people. The light shines in the darkness, and the darkness did not overcome it.

Jn 1:1–5

"In the beginning. . . ."

This Gospel passage is about beginnings. God is good at beginnings. In the beginning the Spirit hovered over the waters and God created the world. In the beginning was the Word and the Word was made flesh and took up residence among us. In the beginning of our Christian life we were baptized, immersed in the water to die and rise with Jesus. Creation. Redemption.

Sanctification. In each case, the people God chose to bless with his beginnings promised fidelity to the covenant God made with them. In each case, including our own, we failed to keep our promises and chose something other than God as the center of our lives. And in each case, including our own, God was right there to set things right, to catch our attention and allure us back to relationship with him. Each day is a new beginning. Each day is another opportunity to discover God who is trying to attract and coax us to a greater love.

I am here, my Lord. I sense that you have something you want to say to me, something special you want to give me. I am ready. I am here. I am here for you.

29 Probe our hearts

Now in Jerusalem by the Sheep Gate there is a pool, called in Hebrew Beth-zatha, which has five porticoes. In these lay many invalids—blind, lame, and paralyzed. One man was there who had been ill for thirty-eight years. When Jesus saw him lying there and knew that he had been there a long time, he said to him, "Do you want to be made well?" The sick man answered him, "Sir, I have no one to put me into the pool when the water is stirred up; and while I am making my way, someone else steps down ahead of me." Jesus said to him, "Stand up, take your mat and walk."

Jn 5:2–8

"Do you want to be made well?"

Jesus is the master of asking the obvious! Who would walk into a hospital where someone has lain for two years in bed, chronically ill, too sick to go home, unresponsive to medical treatments, and ask, "Do you want to get better?" But Jesus did just that! For thirty-eight years this man had been in the portico by the pool waiting to be healed. So why did Jesus ask him what he wanted? Wasn't it obvious? Jesus was probing the man's heart with this simple inquiry. *What do you want?* he asked. Interestingly, the man didn't answer the question. He complained about not having anyone to help him into the water. Jesus cured the man and told him to go home. The man didn't ask to follow Jesus, didn't express gratitude, didn't show the genesis of anything greater in his life than that healing. Neither did Jesus invite the man to accompany him as a disciple. The man didn't know his heart well enough to really know what he wanted in life. And you, what do you most deeply desire for yourself? Your family? The world?

Sadly, my Lord, my heart sometimes lacks passion. At times I don't know what I truly want in life. Have mercy on me.

30 *I need you*

"Two men went up to the temple to pray, one a Pharisee and the other a tax collector. The Pharisee, standing by himself, was praying thus, 'God, I thank you that I am not like other people: thieves, rogues, adulterers, or even like this tax collector. I fast twice a week; I give a tenth of all my income.' But the tax collector, standing far off, would not even look up to heaven, but was beating his breast and saying, 'God, be merciful to me, a sinner!' I tell you, this man went down to his home justified rather than the other; for all who exalt themselves will be humbled, but all who humble themselves will be exalted."

Lk 18:10–14

"But the tax collector, standing far off,
would not even look up to heaven. . . ."

This Gospel reading is like an audiovisual presentation of Matthew's Beatitudes, in which Jesus declares *fortunate* those who have no recourse but God. Luke's parables are stories that can help us understand what Jesus means. There is the widow who cries out for legal justice, and the children who cry out in their unpretentious simplicity for blessing. The rich official cries out for righteousness (though he goes away unable to fulfill its requirements), and the blind man at Jericho cries out his need for only one thing: to see God. Finally, in this selection, we have the tax collector who mourns his sins and cries out for forgiveness. In this chapter, only the Pharisee, a good man and a strict observer of the Law, is not *fortunate*. The Pharisee saw no need to cry out, to reach out of himself and beg God for justice, blessing, mercy, or vision. The Pharisee didn't "get it," because he felt he had in himself everything he wanted or needed. Jesus, instead, came for those who had no one else to depend on but God. Do you need God yet? If you do, you are indeed *fortunate*.

I need you, my God. Accept my heart reaching out to you.

31 *Feelings of insecurity frighten me*

At the approach of Saul and David, on David's return after striking down the Philistine, women came out from all the cities of Israel to meet Saul the king, singing and dancing, with tambourines, joyful songs, and stringed instruments. The women played and sang:
"Saul has slain his thousands,
    and David his tens of thousands."
Saul was very angry and resentful of the song, for he thought: "They give David tens of thousands, but only thousands to me. All that remains for him is the kingship." From that day on, Saul kept a jealous eye on David.

1 Sm 18:6–9 (NABRE)

"Saul was very angry and resentful of the song. . . .
From that day on, Saul kept a jealous eye on David."

It just takes a word that highlights how someone else is better than we, and our insecurity flares up. Especially when we are holding on to something that makes us feel good about ourselves, we can become very touchy and anxious when it is threatened. Basically *all* of us who travel together this rather precarious journey we call life suffer from at least a mild case of insecurity. Every once in a while we are reminded that what we are hanging on to for security could be taken away from us. We discover that the people we thought we lived in solidarity with are actually a threat. Both Saul and David were insecure. Both of them were holding on to the admiration of the crowds. Jonathon, King Saul's son, was a level-headed peacemaker because he was not holding on to anything. He was looking out for the good of both Saul and David. Neither his father nor his friend was a threat to him.

Jesus, feelings of insecurity frighten me. I don't like to feel anxious or jealous. When I feel threatened, send me a Jonathon. Amen.

32 Genuine love

Now that you have purified your souls by your obedience to the truth so that you have genuine mutual love, love one another deeply from the heart. You have been born anew, not of perishable but of imperishable seed, through the living and enduring word of God. For
"All flesh is like grass
and all its glory like the flower of grass.
The grass withers,
and the flower falls,
but the word of the Lord endures forever."
That word is the good news that was announced to you.

1 Pet 1:22–25

> " . . . you have purified your souls . . .
> so that you have genuine mutual love. . . ."

All of us have those times when we just don't agree with others. We may see things differently because of our backgrounds, life experiences, personal agendas, values we hold dear, or, every once in a while, we have to admit, because of just plain obstinacy. In his letter Peter says that we are purified so that we can experience genuine love of one another by *obedience to the truth.* This is such a freeing phrase. Obedience to the truth calls me to become a bigger person. It shapes in me a great heart, and it attracts me to the sacrifices that will create better character in me. Four qualities are necessary to be able to obey the truth: simplicity, sincerity, uprightness, and openness. We must be like a little child who at a certain age is a bundle of wonder. Everything is new! Everything is full of awe and mystery! Such a child is open to all that is true. As adults we can recapture this sense of reverent wonder at what is coming to be, what the possibilities are, the gift of another's values or the other side of the story. We can opt for the humility of listening and waiting and asking.

Transform the smallness of my obstinate hold on my point of view into a large-heartedness modeled after your heart, my God. Mellow me, that I may give the gift of love to all I meet.

33 *We live in Christ*

Now concerning the times and the seasons, brothers and sisters, you do not need to have anything written to you. For you yourselves know very well that the day of the Lord will come like a thief in the night. When they say, "There is peace and security," then sudden destruction will come upon them, as labor pains come upon a pregnant woman, and there will be no escape! But you, beloved, are not in darkness, for that day to surprise you like a thief; for you are all children of light and children of the day; we are not of the night or of darkness.

1 Thess 5:1–5

"For you are all children of light. . . ."

This passage is exultant! St. Paul reminds his beloved Thessalonians that they are now living in this world of light created by the Word! Jesus, the Word of God, is the one whose words divide the light from the dark and create healing and wholeness. His words make things happen! Whether we are alive or have died—and this is the key to Paul and to our own lives—we live *in Christ*. We, individually and as a community, have actually *become* Christ. When the Father looks at us he sees his Son standing in our stead. In the midst of all our problems, whatever they may be, this is what gives us hope. We will never be alone! Jesus cares for each of us as if we were his very own self! We truly are. When times are dark, Jesus has not forgotten you! He can't forget you. Ever. You are *in* him.

Glory be to you, O Father, creator of the day, maker of the light.

34 How God slips into life

Again he entered the synagogue, and a man was there who had a withered hand. They watched him to see whether he would cure him on the sabbath, so that they might accuse him. And he said to the man who had the withered hand, "Come forward." Then he said to them, "Is it lawful to do good or to do harm on the sabbath, to save life or to kill?" But they were silent. He looked around at them with anger; he was grieved at their hardness of heart and said to the man, "Stretch out your hand." He stretched it out, and his hand was restored. The Pharisees went out and immediately conspired with the Herodians against him, how to destroy him.

Mk 3:1–6

" . . . so that they might accuse him."

Reading this Gospel passage, it is easy to forget that it was as a member of the Jewish community that Jesus claimed to have the authority to do what God alone can do—forgive sins. Jesus's activity and teaching must have baffled his contemporaries as they struggled to figure out exactly who he was and why he thought he had the authority to do what he did. Those who watched him carefully in the synagogue that day hoped to gather enough evidence to accuse him. They had lost the open wonder and amazement at God's power, which they had witnessed when Jesus healed the paralytic. Now they were no longer inquirers, observers, or disciples, but his judges. They had made up their minds that what this rabbi had to say couldn't possibly be from God. It is so easy for me to slip from being disciple to judge. Every time I put myself, my comfort, my ideas, my excuses before obedience I am no longer a disciple, but have put myself in the place of judging the worth of Jesus's teaching and examples. I forget that God slips into my life in baffling ways, turning my values and judgments on their head.

Lord, help me to remain amazed and not angered by you who interfere with my pride and my plans, trusting that you know what you desire to make of me and how you plan to use me. Amen.

35 *Our utter glory is obedience*

The people spoke against God and against Moses, "Why have you brought us up out of Egypt to die in the wilderness? For there is no food and no water, and we detest this miserable food." Then the LORD sent poisonous serpents among the people, and they bit the people, so that many Israelites died. The people came to Moses and said, "We have sinned by speaking against the LORD and against you; pray to the LORD to take away the serpents from us." So Moses prayed for the people. And the LORD said to Moses, "Make a poisonous serpent, and set it on a pole; and everyone who is bitten shall look at it and live."

Num 21:5–8

"The people spoke against God. . . ."

This passage has long been one of my favorites. As I grow older it has knit its way into the fiber of my soul and character. In the exchange between the people and Moses that dry, dusty day, I don't think it was the food and water that created all the havoc with the snakes.

It was the power of their wills and the direction they were pointed that made all the difference. If our wills are pointed toward self, then something as small as a drink of water can precipitate a big argument. There are a hundred reasons to demand the water *now*. If our wills are pointed toward God, in a relationship of responsibility toward truth and goodness, and under the authority of another, we discover freedom and receive glory even in the case of humiliation and failure. Our wills are always in relation to another's. *God* loved us, *God* sent his Son: we obey in freedom and love. May we recognize as we grow older that it is this letting go of how we need to have things done that opens the way to discover what Jesus came to show us: the utter glory of the human creature is obedience.

Obedience can be a hard word, Lord, until I remember that you have led the way even in this. You, the obedient Son of the Father, have made all obedience fruitful. Help me to follow you. Amen.

36 We are powerless

After [Jesus] had finished speaking, he said to Simon, "Put out into deep water and lower your nets for a catch." Simon said in reply, "Master, we have worked hard all night and have caught nothing, but at your command I will lower the nets." When they had done this, they caught a great number of fish and their nets were tearing. . . . When Simon Peter saw this, he fell at the knees of Jesus and said, "Depart from me, Lord, for I am a sinful man." . . . Jesus said to Simon, "Do not be afraid; from now on you will be catching men."

Lk 5:4–6, 8, 10 (NABRE)

"Depart from me, Lord. . . ."

Poor Peter! He's just been overwhelmed by the magnificent generosity of God. All of a sudden he has realized *who* is in his boat. It would be like a taxi cab driver stopping at the scene of an accident and witnessing his passenger miraculously bring someone back from the dead. Whoa! Often our first reaction when we witness a remarkable manifestation of God's presence and love is to create distance. I think it is because such experiences make it clear to us on a very deep level that we are actually not as powerful as we think we are. Like Peter—the professional fisherman who couldn't force the fish into his net but discovered that someone else could fill his nets on command—we realize our small-ness and poverty in the midst of a creation so vast it can't be controlled or explained. We are indeed powerless in the face of so many things in life. Jesus wants to work miracles for you, in your boat, where you live and work today—miracles that will help you see what he wants to do in your life and the mission he has given you. Stay awake!

Come, Jesus, into my boat. I long to be surprised by your generosity today. I long to witness the evidence of your care for me. Come!

37 Humility

My brothers and sisters, do you with your acts of favor-
itism really believe in our glorious Lord Jesus Christ?
For if a person with gold rings and in fine clothes comes
into your assembly, and if a poor person in dirty clothes
also comes in, and if you take notice of the one wear-
ing the fine clothes and say, "Have a seat here, please,"
while to the one who is poor you say, "Stand there," or,
"Sit at my feet," have you not made distinctions among
yourselves, and become judges with evil thoughts? . . .
For judgment will be without mercy to anyone who
has shown no mercy; mercy triumphs over judgment.

Jas 2:1–4, 13

" . . . mercy triumphs over judgment."

I have recently learned how important it is to lay on
the table what I know, or think I know, and allow it to
be measured by the experiences and insights of others.
There is a sneaky trick the evil spirit plays, convincing
me I don't need others, leading me to a protective isolation, making me afraid of someone else's sharp mind, or

defensive of my own way of Christian living. What starts out as fear ends as prejudice. This passage from James seems so blatant that it almost doesn't strike home. I would probably never speak to a poor person in the way James describes; poverty more often than not draws forth compassion. However, I would be wise to admit that I do think this way about people who threaten me or cause me anxiety. These people are not financially poor, but, in my insecurity, I paint them as poor in virtue, poor in intelligence, poor in personal talent.

Lord, convince me of my poverty so that I can trust you entirely with my life. Free me from anxiety so that I can trust the gifts of others. Save me from prejudice so that together with others, I may seek you in humility and mutual love. Amen.

38 *God's love saves me!*

For God so loved the world that he gave his only Son, so that everyone who believes in him may not perish but may have eternal life. Indeed, God did not send the Son into the world to condemn the world, but in order that the world might be saved through him. Those who believe in him are not condemned; but those who do not believe are condemned already, because they have not believed in the name of the only Son of God.

Jn 3:16–18

"God did not send the Son into the world to condemn the world,
but in order that the world might be saved through him."

Often the straightest way to the meaning of the text is *experiencing* the text. On retreat this year, for the first time, I experienced what the words of this passage mean. For the first readers of John's Gospel, the Greek *sōzō*, meaning *to save*, had the powerful sense of deliverance from a particularly *perilous* situation, or from a mortal danger. Kneeling in chapel, after celebrating the sacrament of Reconciliation, I was overwhelmed with a knowledge from the inside out that I had been rescued, delivered, protected, that someone had grabbed my hand just as I was slipping away, that I had been brought out of harm's way when I had no way to save myself. This is what Jesus is all about. God refused to give up on us. He handed over the dearest possession a Father could have, his only Son, so that we would be brought up into God's embrace and lifted to a place of rest, of love, of belonging, and of mercy.

God, you sent your Son not to definitively sever any friendship or responsibility you might have in our regard. No. You sent your Son to rescue us because you can do nothing less than remain faithful to your covenant of love forever.

39 *Love always triumphs*

Thus says the LORD:
I am going to restore the fortunes of the tents of Jacob,
    and have compassion on his dwellings. . . .
Their prince shall be one of their own,
    their ruler shall come from their midst;
I will bring him near, and he shall approach me,
    for who would otherwise dare to approach me?
    says the LORD.
And you shall be my people,
    and I will be your God.

Jer 30:18, 21–22

"And you shall be my people, and I will be your God."

This is an astonishing commitment of love! Astonishing because it is not promised to people who have proven themselves worthy of such recognition from God. Rather, Jeremiah clearly states that the peoples' sin was so grievous that their wound was incurable, that for them there was no hope for healing, that there was no relief in sight for their pain. Such cruel words could only come from a broken heart. Often Scripture portrays God as brokenhearted at the disloyalty of his people. He abandons them to their own devices and exile. But love, even when betrayed, still triumphs. "I am going to restore the fortunes of the tents of Jacob. . . ." No matter what we've done, no matter how awful the circumstances of our lives may be that could cause us to cry out against God, love will triumph in the end because God will not let us go. We are his people and he is our God.

Do not let me go, my God. Hold on to me even when I would run away. Let your love conquer me! I claim you as my God, for you have claimed me as your child.

40 _Taken apart and rebuilt_

In the days of his flesh, Jesus offered up prayers and supplications, with loud cries and tears, to the one who was able to save him from death, and he was heard because of his reverent submission. Although he was a Son, he learned obedience through what he suffered; and having been made perfect, he became the source of eternal salvation for all who obey him, having been designated by God a high priest according to the order of Melchizedek.

Heb 5:7–10

_" . . . he learned obedience through what he suffered,
and having been made perfect. . . ."_

We all know the wise advice: "Practice makes perfect." If we study hard, we can get a perfect score on a test. If we pay attention to detail and have a creative vision, we can execute the perfect project. If we are careful who we hire, we can create the perfect team. We'll climb the corporate ladder if we do things right and avoid any misstep. Books tell parents how to raise perfect kids. Perfection creates a lot of pressure. In the end, it's an illusion. I am grateful I learned early on through serious sickness that real "perfection" comes through suffering: through darkness faced, disaster overcome, temptation endured, sickness surmounted or surrendered to. When one has been taken apart and rebuilt through this process, then "perfection" does roll off our fingers: a perfection that is received. I don't need to achieve or accomplish anything to be perfect. I only need to surrender to what God is doing in me and through me in the world. It may look "perfect" according to others, or it may appear as a complete disaster like the crucifixion of Jesus. In either case, as long as God is glorified, it is perfectly fine with me.

Accomplish your will in me, my God. Right now I embrace whatever your will may be. With all my heart I desire it. Amen.

PART III

Do Not Be Afraid; I Am with You

41 *I forbid you to fear*

Immediately he made the disciples get into the boat and go on ahead to the other side, while he dismissed the crowds. And after he had dismissed the crowds, he went up the mountain by himself to pray. When evening came, he was there alone, but by this time the boat, battered by the waves, was far from the land, for the wind was against them. And early in the morning he came walking toward them on the sea. But when the disciples saw him walking on the sea, they were terrified, saying, "It is a ghost!" And they cried out in fear. But immediately Jesus spoke to them and said, "Take heart, it is I; do not be afraid."

Mt 14:22–27

"But immediately Jesus spoke to them and said,
'Take heart, it is I; do not be afraid.'"

A friend of mine speaks, somewhat resentfully, about her pains: "Jesus suffered, so that means I have to suffer too." The disciples' cry of fear from the midst of a situation that threatens destruction would be just another one of those proofs that we can't expect anything better of life than suffering. Somehow, however, this type of reasoning makes God at once the cause of evil and the One who has no power or desire to save us. What we see in this Gospel passage, instead, is the divine way in which God turns the tables on his disciples to teach us to see things from the divine perspective. From the center of a situation of fear and danger—a situation that he has allowed in their lives—Jesus does two things. First Jesus states, *I forbid you to go on fearing from this point forward* (a more accurate translation of the Greek), and second, he *approaches* the boat. Jesus walks straight toward us in our personal crisis into the *midst* of the fearful situation. God shows us that his love is more powerful than the dangers around us, and in our sufferings we can discover him taking up his abode in our frightened hearts and commanding, "Do not be afraid!"

Come, Jesus, right into the midst of my struggles. In every crisis may I see you and fear no more.

42 *The vision has its time*

Are you not from of old, O LORD,
    my holy God, immortal?
LORD, you have appointed them for judgment,
    O Rock, you have set them in place to punish!
Your eyes are too pure to look upon wickedness,
    and the sight of evil you cannot endure.
Why, then, do you gaze on the faithless in silence
    while the wicked devour those more just than
    themselves?

Hab 1:12–13 (NABRE)

"Why, then, do you gaze on the faithless in silence
while the wicked devour those more just than themselves?"

At any one point how many millions are probably saying these very words to God? People who have been swindled of their money, seen loved ones lose life or limb because of another's careless or criminal activity, had to forfeit career or reputation, or been left with psychological wounds too terrible to bear from another's sinful behavior. Why, O God, do you sit by and do nothing to protect your loved ones? The next lines of this passage are perhaps the only answer: "For the vision still has its time . . . if it delays, wait for it, it will surely come . . . the just man, because of his faith, shall live" (Hab 2:2–4). Jesus himself, hanging on the cross, had to wait for God's vindication. He surrendered his life in complete trust that his Father loved him despite the fact that all he could see was that he was left alone in the most pitiable of circumstances. Three days he lay in the darkness of the tomb. Then God raised him up in glory. Jesus proved to us that God can be trusted. We can be sure, no matter what has gone wrong in our lives, that "the just man, because of his faith, shall live" (Hab 2:4).

My heart breaks when I see another suffer and often I have no words to say. Sometimes my own faith in you, my God, is shaken. Strengthen my belief in you!

43 The riddle of our existence

Blessed be the Lord God of Israel,
>   for he has looked favorably on his people and
>   redeemed them.
He has raised up a mighty savior for us
>   in the house of his servant David,
as he spoke through the mouth of his holy prophets from
of old,
>   that we would be saved from our enemies and from
>   the hand of all who hate us.
Thus he has shown the mercy promised to our ancestors,
>   and has remembered his holy covenant,
the oath that he swore to our ancestor Abraham. . . .

Lk 1:68–73

" . . . he has looked favorably on his people and redeemed them."

The words of this Gospel reveal a lot about God's stance toward the work of his creative love. They are words of *mercy* and words of *action*. Sometimes we wonder where God is. Those who bear great sorrow in their hearts can often find themselves overwhelmed by questions and loneliness. Where is God? What does it all mean? Zechariah's canticle, however, proclaims that God *is* mercy and action. God never promised to rescue his people from the human condition. Instead he did something so wondrous we could never comprehend it: he came to *share* our human condition *with us*. He was born. He grew up. He suffered. He was betrayed. He was alone. He died. And he rose from death and ascended into heaven *where we are now able to follow.*

Jesus, you showed us that what we *experience* as the human condition does not contain the key to the riddle of our existence. Only Love does. Help us to gradually become strong enough to love even in the midst of disappointment and pain. May we share in the power of your salvific love, that we might discover the ultimate meaning of our lives.

44 *The reason I'm still alive*

The LORD is my shepherd, I shall not want.
    He makes me lie down in green pastures;
he leads me beside still waters;
    he restores my soul.
He leads me in right paths
    for his name's sake.
Even though I walk through the darkest valley,
    I fear no evil;
for you are with me;
    your rod and your staff—
    they comfort me.
. . . Surely goodness and mercy shall follow me
    all the days of my life,
and I shall dwell in the house of the LORD
    my whole life long.

Ps 23:1–4, 6

"Surely goodness and mercy shall follow me all the days of my life."

I speak often with a mother, Sarah, whose husband turned her and their two girls out of their home in order to marry another woman. Sarah spent almost a year in homeless shelters with her children, gradually earning enough money to move to another town, find new schools for her children, and buy a small house. Only one thing gets her out of bed in the morning—her children. Psalm 23 is one of her favorite psalms: *The Lord is my shepherd. . . . He leads me, he restores my soul, he guides me, he gives me courage, he anoints me, and I shall live with him forever.* The psalmist declares his unshakeable faith in the love of God for him, "even though I walk through the darkest valley." Sarah has learned this lesson well. I am moved when she tells me how much God loves her, that she knows it is only God who has helped her survive all she has been through: "He is the reason I am still alive." She declares her faith in him in the midst of the chaos. From the psalmist and from Sarah, I've learned that adoration and self-abandonment are the truly Christian response to the vicissitudes of our life journey.

I thank you, my Lord, for all those who witness to your fidelity as they walk through dark valleys. They are a gift to me.

45 *The Lord comes in strength*

"Everyone then who hears these words of mine and acts on them will be like a wise man who built his house on rock. The rain fell, the floods came, and the winds blew and beat on that house, but it did not fall, because it had been founded on rock. And everyone who hears these words of mine and does not act on them will be like a foolish man who built his house on sand. The rain fell, and the floods came, and the winds blew and beat against that house, and it fell—and great was its fall!"

Mt 7:24–27

"The rain fell, the floods came,
and the winds blew and beat on that house. . . ."

Raise your voice and tell the Good News: the Lord our God comes in strength! This Gospel passage about the rainy season, with the torrents and winds that tested the houses of both the wise and foolish, is an image of strength. I hear accounts of these torrents and winds in people's lives over and over again, every single day: financial difficulties, unexpected illnesses, relationship failures, employment problems. Indeed, the Gospel's rainy season comes to each of our lives at one time or another. Whether we are in that season right now or not, we need to test the foundation of our lives. Is it strong? Has the "house" of our life been built on the solid rock of faith and obedient love? The torrents and winds come crashing into life in this fallen world, but the Good News is that as strong as they may blow, and as hard as they may buffet our hearts, the Lord our God is stronger! Truly, "we have a strong city" (Isa 26:1).

Lord, it is true. My life has seen strong winds and torrential downpours that I feared would destroy me. But you were stronger. I praise you forever.

46 Transforming disaster into life

After saying this Jesus was troubled in spirit, and declared, "Very truly, I tell you, one of you will betray me." . . . "Lord, who is it?" Jesus answered, "It is the one to whom I give this piece of bread when I have dipped it in the dish." So when he had dipped the piece of bread, he gave it to Judas son of Simon Iscariot. After he received the piece of bread, Satan entered into him. Jesus said to him, "Do quickly what you are going to do."

Jn 13:21, 25–27

"Do quickly what you are going to do."

It is instinctive for humans to seek to preserve their life. We marvel at and give honors to persons who put their life in jeopardy to save another. In this Gospel passage, Jesus steps out of the very human pattern of self-preservation and we almost miss it. Jesus sees the dark clouds gathering on the horizon. Yet Jesus gives Judas permission to leave the table and go into the night to accomplish the plans he harbors in his heart. Jesus lets him go. No persuasion to change his mind. No last-minute attempts to win Judas over. No underhanded statements to alert the other apostles to the impending catastrophe. Jesus simply tells Judas to go and accomplish his plans quickly. What must Jesus have felt as his eyes followed this hand-picked apostle with whom he had shared so many blessed experiences over the past three years? Jesus watched sadly as the man rose from the table, looked furtively around, and backed out of the room, closing the door firmly behind him. At times we are in a similar predicament. A painful situation enters our life and with dignity we live it fully, trusting in the Father's overarching goodness, which alone can transform disaster into life.

Today I take a moment to connect the dots in my life—yes, Lord, you have been good. The painful moments and days have left me with a treasure. The darkness has led me to light and life. Thank you.

47 *Allow Mary to hold you*

Guided by the Spirit, Simeon came into the temple;
and when the parents brought in the child Jesus, to do
for him what was customary under the law, Simeon
took him in his arms and praised God. . . . And the
child's father and mother were amazed at what was
being said about him. Then Simeon blessed them and
said to his mother Mary, "This child is destined for the
falling and the rising of many in Israel, and to be a sign
that will be opposed so that the inner thoughts of
many will be revealed—and a sword will pierce your
own soul too."

Lk 2:27–28, 33–35

" . . . *a sword will pierce your own soul too.*"

Our grown children suffer from depression, bully-
ing, eating disorders, divorce, loneliness, financial
disaster. . . . The list could go on and on. But for a mother's heart it is more than a list. It is the prospect of her
child's life swirling out of control, of the family's attention and resources being swallowed up by the incalculable

and unforgiveable. Mary's heart, in the temple where she presented her Son to the Lord, was also shaken by the vision of what form that "sword" could take. She walked with her child through the joys and pains of his life, and stood before the "failure" and utter disappointment of the crucifixion. Mary, like every sorrowful mother, somehow had the faith to believe in her Son even as she held his dead body and laid it in a grave. To believe, yes, and with oh so much love to hold the image of his face in her heart. She, above all women, knows a mother's sorrows. If you are sorrowing or you know a mother who is, pick up a life of the Blessed Mother, your rosary, the Scriptures, and allow her to hold you, as only a mother can, in your sorrow.

I take you, Mary, to be my mother. Walk with me in the joys and sorrows of my life. Amen.

48 *God alone saves*

Blessed be the LORD, my rock,
>   who trains my hands for war, and my fingers
>   for battle;
my rock and my fortress,
>   my stronghold and my deliverer,
my shield, in whom I take refuge,
>   who subdues the peoples under me.
O LORD, what are human beings that you regard them,
>   or mortals that you think of them?
They are like a breath;
>   their days are like a passing shadow.

Ps 144:1–4

"My rock and my fortress, my stronghold and my deliverer,
my shield, in whom I take refuge. . . ."

Tragedy is never far from the human condition. We experience it personally and we live through tragic times as a family, community, or nation. Fear, illness, depression, abuse, and financial disaster are at our heels. We fend them off, look for lucky breaks, try whatever will keep us beyond their reach. Sometimes prayer can be reduced to asking for help for ourselves, our families, friends, and neighbors. This psalm offers us a way to pray in those tragic times. It begins with the king stating his dependence on God. God is a safeguard, our fortress, our stronghold, our deliverer. We can trust God. God is the one who gives kings their victory. God will rescue. These words were no doubt written at a time of crisis that threatened the future of the king and the people. I have seen people go through tremendous times of pain and crisis. The only thing that we can know to be true at those moments is that God *is* faithful. That God alone saves. That God walks with us through our dark valleys and hangs with us on our crosses. We wait for God to appear, only to discover that he is already with us and we are not alone. In our deepest pain we can trust that he is working to save.

O faithful Love, walk with me through both sorrow and joy. Let me see your face and I shall be saved.

49 Keep watch

I will stand at my watchpost,
    and station myself on the rampart;
I will keep watch to see what he will say to me,
    and what he will answer concerning my complaint.
Then the LORD answered me and said:
Write the vision;
    make it plain on tablets. . . .
For there is still a vision for the appointed time;
    it speaks of the end, and does not lie.
If it seems to tarry, wait for it;
    it will surely come, it will not delay.
Look at the proud!
    Their spirit is not right in them,
    but the righteous live by their faith.

Hab 2:1–4

"I will stand at my watchpost . . . I will keep watch to see what he will say to me, and what he will answer concerning my complaint."

Habakkuk became a prophet when the Israelites were struggling with a desperate situation. In this passage, Habakkuk complains to God, and then says, *All right, I am going to see how the Lord responds. I am going to sit here until I get an answer.* The prophet dares to address God with boldness and assurance.

While reflecting on Habakkuk's prayer, I received a phone call from a woman who often asks for prayers. She told me she had only $10 left in her wallet. An abusive husband had left her with no home and no sense of self-worth. She had no job. She was afraid. Desperate. Lonely. She was in a place of insecurity the depth of which I will probably never experience. After talking and praying together, we could say only one thing. *We shall station ourselves at our post and see what God does.* It's easy to trust God when a financial cushion separates us from living on the streets. In this desperate situation, however, can God *really* come through? When the rubber meets the road, does God *really* care about us? These questions tear at the souls of Christians today. As the rich become richer and the poor become more desperate, where is God for them, for us? How will God save? *Let us see what the Lord will do. Let us wait here until we get an answer.*

Lord of the vision, promise of the future, come, do not tarry.

50 Do not be troubled

"Do not let your hearts be troubled. Believe in God, believe also in me. In my Father's house there are many dwelling places. If it were not so, would I have told you that I go to prepare a place for you? And if I go and prepare a place for you, I will come again and will take you to myself, so that where I am, there you may be also. And you know the way to the place where I am going." Thomas said to him, "Lord we do not know where you are going. How can we know the way?" Jesus said to him, "I am the way, and the truth, and the life."

Jn 14:1–6

"I am the way, and the truth, and the life."

All of revelation has as its goal the manifestation of God's glory. Jesus discloses to us the Father's glory and we are entranced by what we see: his goodness, his wisdom, his healing love. When we enter into the story of Jesus, we become absorbed by it and come to know the God who is love revealed in Jesus his Son. The Spirit of Jesus blows through salvation history, making the life, death, and resurrection of Jesus contemporaneous with each age of the Church. Through the Spirit's work, Jesus himself is the one who reveals to each of us today the utter truth of God's glory. In so doing he reveals to us our own glory. He is the way to become good, as God is good, not through any successful imitation on our part, but because God has sent his Son to do what we could not do for ourselves. Jesus alone can stand before God as good, because he became flesh and died for us so that we might be incorporated into the glory and beauty of the Father, fountain of life and love. In him, we stand before the Father as good.

Jesus, Master, Way, Truth, and Life, draw my heart to the true, the good, and the beautiful that I might be taken up into the greatness of your Father's plan which wildly exceeds all I could dream or imagine.

51 We depend on miracles

Then suddenly a woman who had been suffering from hemorrhages for twelve years came up behind him and touched the fringe of his cloak, for she said to herself, "If I only touch his cloak, I will be made well." Jesus turned, and seeing her he said, "Take heart, daughter; your faith has made you well." And instantly the woman was made well.

Mt 9:20–22

" . . . a woman . . . came up behind him. . . ."

This unnamed woman who approaches Jesus with her need symbolizes each of us. We too are totally dependent on miracles. We can't heal ourselves. We can't fix our problems. Just like this woman, we seek help from doctors and experts in so many areas—medicine, psychology, science, physics, strategic planning, government, law, education, time management, and the list goes on. Each has their place. Each contributes something wonderful to the development of this world. But in the end, we must approach God as the ultimate power of love which alone can sustain our existence. Our existence rests on the hands of grace. Of ourselves we can only really *receive* life and give thanks for it as a continuous gift. Our most authentic posture as a part of God's creation is that of this woman suffering from hemorrhages: "If only I can touch him, I shall be saved." It is her faith, her courage, her determination, her risk to show her need, her desire for health, and her realization of God's infinite superiority over the world that we must claim for our own if we are to receive, like her, true healing and life.

Infinite Love of our God! If only I could know you, if only I could touch you, I would be healed!

52 *Touching God's presence*

In the sixth month the angel Gabriel was sent by God to a town in Galilee called Nazareth, to a virgin engaged to a man whose name was Joseph, of the house of David. The virgin's name was Mary. . . . The angel said to her, "Do not be afraid, Mary, for you have found favor with God. And now, you will conceive in your womb and bear a son, and you will name him Jesus. He will be great, and will be called the Son of the Most High, and the Lord God will give to him the throne of his ancestor David. He will reign over the house of Jacob forever, and of his kingdom there will be no end."

Lk 1:26–27, 30–33

"And now, you will conceive in your womb and bear a son, and you will name him Jesus."

A woman recently said to me, "You seem to be able to touch God's presence as if it were real." *AS IF it were real!* Without realizing it, she had put into words our modern anguish that God seems so remote. He seems to be nothing more than invisible gas—a ghostly non-reality, a deity without the face or voice we long to see and hear. This modern conception of God is far from the God whose Son became Mary's baby—personal, compassionate, involved, committed to us. This Gospel passage speaks of visions of angels, messages from God, commitments of faith, obedient adoration: all things that can easily be brushed off as the uninformed piety of the simple minded. After all, science and technology think they know what *really* makes the world go round. This Gospel, however, puts us square in the realm of the reality that only the faith of the simple can see. God is as real and involved in our lives as when he asked Mary to be the mother of his Son.

Mary, show us God's face once more. Teach us to hear his voice again and again. Amen.

53 A tidal wave of love

And when they came to a place called Golgotha (which means Place of a Skull), they offered him wine to drink, mixed with gall; but when he tasted it, he would not drink it. And when they had crucified him, they divided his clothes among themselves by casting lots; then they sat down there and kept watch over him. Over his head they put the charge against him, which read, "This is Jesus, the King of the Jews." . . . From noon on, darkness came over the whole land until three in the afternoon. And about three o'clock Jesus cried with a loud voice," . . . My God, my God, why have you forsaken me?" Then Jesus cried again with a loud voice and breathed his last.

Mt 27:33–37, 45–46, 50

"[Jesus] breathed his last."

Jesus, crucified and forsaken on the cross, shows us the extent to which we are called to love. He is the image of what the divine dance of love in the Trinity is: it is total, all-embracing, completely self-forgetful, vulnerable gift. We cannot see the Persons of the Trinity in their relationships with one another, but we *can* see how we have been loved by Jesus, the Incarnate Son of God. Jesus came and carried all the weight of our burden. He took upon himself not only our sin, but our death, our experience of frustrated relationships, our alienation, our forsakenness. He did not love us with a sterile love from afar. He touched us and held us. He nursed us back to health with the healing balm of his death and paid the price of our salvation with his own blood. What would happen if we loved one another this way? It is hard, I must admit. Efficiency, the bottom line, advantage, and personal plans have to give way, have to crumble before the onslaught of this tidal wave of love. But, oh, how much more blessed and fulfilled would our lives be? And the world? Would it not be a much more beautiful place to live?

From this point, Lord, I resolve to live a life of total, self-forgetful gift. May my love contribute to peace in the world.

54 Keep on loving

Now as [Saul] was going along and approaching Damascus, suddenly a light from heaven flashed around him. He fell to the ground and heard a voice saying to him, "Saul, Saul, why do you persecute me?" He asked, "Who are you, Lord?" The reply came, "I am Jesus, whom you are persecuting. But get up and enter the city, and you will be told what you are to do." . . . Saul got up from the ground, and though his eyes were open, he could see nothing. . . . So Ananias went and . . . laid his hands on Saul and said, "Brother Saul, the Lord Jesus, who appeared to you on your way here, has sent me so that you may regain your sight and be filled with the Holy Spirit."

Acts 9:3–6, 8, 17–18

" . . . you will be told what to do."

Paul is loved without limit. Paul responds by loving without limit. It's not that he went blazing through the world accomplishing a great project he had developed to prove his love for God. God wouldn't allow him to make that mistake! On the road to Damascus where

God revealed Jesus to Paul, he said: *I have this vocation for you, Paul. Go into the city and there you will be told about it.* God sent Paul to the community of Christians, the very people he had come to imprison, the followers of the Way whom he had despised. Jesus incorporated him into this community not as a celebrated hero, but as the least, as one accepted though not worthy, as one forgiven and reconciled. Jesus made him wait. Jesus made him dependent. Jesus let him experience the love of the Christian community, as well as the friction, as he sought to carry out the evangelization of the Gentiles. In the midst of his everyday experience, Paul kept loving. This is his message to us. Different events and situations punctuate our days and shape our lives. Our business is to keep loving. In chaos . . . love. In misunderstandings . . . love. In affection . . . love in Christ. In joy and in sorrow . . . love. Always love. Love in all things. Love more. Never stop loving.

Show me, Lord, how I can love more. When my heart wants to shrivel in sorrow, jealousy, or anger, open it to the horizons and rewards of love.

55 Two things we can trust

Now the whole earth had one language and the same words. And . . . they came upon a plain in the land of Shinar and settled there. Then they said, "Come, let us build ourselves a city, and a tower with its top in the heavens, and let us make a name for ourselves. . . ." The LORD came down to see the city and the tower, which mortals had built. And the LORD said, "Look, they are one people, and they have all one language . . . nothing that they propose to do will now be impossible for them. Come, let us go down, and confuse their language there, so that they will not understand one another's speech." So the LORD scattered them abroad . . . and they left off building the city.

Gen 11:1–2, 4–8

"Come, let us go down, and confuse their language there. . . ."

The people building the city of Babel were a bit pretentious, planning to build their lives and their city on their own and for their own ends. If we are honest, however, probably all of us have fallen into this very human tendency. Often when we are forced to stop because of sickness, failure, or obstacles, we begin to resonate with deeper values and our life has more meaning. God leaves us with something beautiful even as he prevents us from building our own lives and cities without him.

But this is not the end of the story. In the Acts of the Apostles, after the Spirit descended upon Mary and the apostles, Peter spoke to those gathered in Jerusalem. All of these people who spoke different languages were able to understand Peter's message (cf. Acts 2). Now *God* was building the city, and continuing to live in our midst through the Spirit. At times we cannot understand why God has let something happen. We can always trust two things, however: first, there is something we can learn no matter how unfair the situation; and second, if we allow God to "build the city," we do not have to be afraid because God will work things out for our good.

Lord, direct my life. Free me from the pride that would lead me to build up my life for my own glory. Help me instead to live for you. Amen.

56 Build up the body of Christ

> For just as the body is one and has many members, and all the members of the body, though many, are one body, so it is with Christ. For in the one Spirit we were all baptized into one body—Jews or Greeks, slaves or free—and we were all made to drink of one Spirit.
>
> . . . Now you are the body of Christ and individually members of it.

1 Cor 12:12–13, 27

" . . . all the members of the body. . . ."

Together we are Christ in the world. Together. A tough word. It would be easier to do it one by one, individually, alone, on my own time, in my own style, to my own end. But we can't get away from that little word: together. We are all members of one body, and that body is Christ. This means that whenever one of us is present to another, Christ is present. When someone ministers to us, Christ is ministering. When I teach someone,

Christ is teaching. We do not need to be afraid of conflicts. They are created by our struggles to grow in maturity and to overcome individualism, collectivism, isolation, and self-serving agendas. These conflicts sand away the sharp edges of our characters and transform our selfishness until the body can live together as one, in harmony, in mutual obedience, growing in love and freedom. Each of us is not simply a cell in the body of Christ. Each of us individually and together is Christ's body. Each of us can build up the body of Christ within ourselves, for the sake of others, in the Church and in service to the world.

How can it be that I—and each of us— have been raised to the honor of being members of the body of Christ? For this, Lord, I praise you.

57 *Where to look for Jesus*

[O]n that same day two of them were going to a village called Emmaus, about seven miles from Jerusalem, and talking with each other about all these things that had happened. While they were talking and discussing, Jesus himself came near and went with them, but their eyes were kept from recognizing him. . . . Then he said to them, "Oh, how foolish you are, and how slow of heart to believe all that the prophets have declared!" Then beginning with Moses and all the prophets, he interpreted to them the things about himself in all the scriptures. . . .

When he was at the table with them, he took bread, blessed and broke it, and gave it to them. Then their eyes were opened, and they recognized him. . . .

Lk 24:13–16, 25, 27, 30–31

"Jesus himself came near and went with them. . . ."

It is such a grace that the Gospel of Luke gives us this account! Without it, how would we know where to look for Jesus? All that we read prior to the resurrection recounts people coming to Jesus when they could see him, and hear him, and physically grasp his hand. But what about those of us who live after Jesus's ascension? How will we know where to find him? How can we hear him? St. Luke's account of the two disciples teaches me three lessons about finding Jesus. First, on my own, like the two disciples, the best I can do is attempt to figure things out. Jesus meets me on the road I am walking. He will reveal to me a different way of seeing things: the way of faith. Second, Jesus tells me not to be afraid of the crises I or others experience. They will all, like the crucifixion, one day be mysteriously taken up and trans-figured in a manner none of us can know right now. Third, we will find Jesus always, whenever we need him, in the breaking of the bread. Jesus specifically left us the Eucharist so that he would be here with us always and we would be able to find him.

Jesus, our Life, come to meet us. When we are con-fused, lost, or discouraged, come alongside us. Draw us to the breaking of the bread.

58 Remembering the promise

His divine power has given us everything needed for life and godliness, through the knowledge of him who called us by his own glory and goodness. Thus he has given us . . . his precious and very great promises, so that through them you may escape from the corruption that is in the world because of lust, and may become participants of the divine nature. For this very reason, you must make every effort to support your faith with goodness, and goodness with knowledge, and knowledge with self-control, and self-control with endurance, and endurance with godliness, and godliness with mutual affection, and mutual affection with love. . . . For anyone who lacks these things is near-sighted and blind, and is forgetful of the cleansing of past sins.

2 Pet 1:3–7, 9

" . . . he has given us . . . his precious and very great promises. . . ."

This passage is a kind of "scrapbook" that memorializes the various facets of our Christian life. Do you keep a "spiritual scrapbook"? We can too quickly lose track of the "precious and very great promises" that we have received, promises that would lead to a changed life, to a life of goodness and love and holiness, to the complete living of our call and election. Perhaps it was a grace received on our first Communion day or wedding day. Perhaps it was a silent movement of our soul or an invitation of grace, received when someone had given us their time or been there for us when no one else was around. A sunset, a baby's smile, a funeral, our child's graduation, a quiet morning working in the garden, a prayer meeting, Eucharistic adoration. . . . God can move in our lives even in the most unexpected places. Take a moment to remember these times, to "scrapbook" them mentally. What was the invitation? What was the gift? What was the beauty of those moments? We are, indeed, given everything we need for a life of godliness, if we remember these precious treasures and "very great promises."

How quickly I forget, my Lord, your visits in my life. Impress on my heart and burn into my soul the vision of your face, the memory of your words to me . . . *to me*.

59 *To love is to risk*

For God is love.

1 Jn 4:8

" . . . *love*. . . . "

Love is the life of God. We came forth from loving hands. We were mercifully clothed in the garden after we had broken God's trust. We have been pursued by Love, collectively and individually. Love died as nothing on the cross, transferring to us the gift of the Father's love. We have been bought at a price by Love for love. If we truly live, we live of love. If we are truly human, we are love. Love, human and divine, is fragile. Its only power is the power of forgiveness, the power of those who wait, who search, who desire. It is not the power of military might, commerce, or lust. Love plays a different song. Trusting love's music is hard. The song of Love can be threatened by the cacophony of fear, insecurity, and need. The wall of love's edifice is cracked and the foundation of love is eroded by the enticements of power and security. To love is to risk. Not to love is to risk even more. It is a choice, a choice to forgive, to give to a selfish person, to be with an older person who needs a friend, to work on a relationship with a friend or spouse. Loving is the life of God . . . loving is authentic living.

Jesus, lover of all humanity, Love of my soul, break the shell of my boredom that I might be love in the world.

60 Broken for love of others

Then he took a loaf of bread, and when he had given thanks, he broke it and gave it to them, saying, "This is my body, which is given for you. Do this in remembrance of me." And he did the same with the cup after supper, saying, "This cup that is poured out for you is the new covenant in my blood."

Lk 22:19–20

"This is my body. . . ."

At Mass—the eucharistic sacrifice, the loving last meal of Jesus celebrated again and again as the agape, the self-giving love, of the Christian community—we are there for each other. I remember being told on the day we practiced for our first Communion, "Don't look around. If I catch any of you looking around. . . ." I forget the consequences of this offense, but it was enough to keep me from looking around during Mass for years to come. Lately, however, I've come to question the wisdom of this advice. Though it may be appropriate for second graders to curtail their distraction and not look around at Mass, it may not be wise advice for adults. I would say, "Look around the next time you go to Mass. You are there for others. You are there for the world." When the priest comes to the words of consecration listen carefully. "This is my body," he says. The words of Jesus. We are called to say to one another: *This is my body, laid on the altar with Christ, broken for love of you, given over to your service, transformed by loving kindness.*

Jesus, each Sunday I witness again true love, I receive anew Love made flesh, I am shaped once more by your love, a love that is out of this world. Each week help me start afresh to give myself to others in loving service.

PART IV

Trust in the Lord with All Your Heart

61 *Have absolute confidence*

And when he got into the boat, his disciples followed him. A windstorm arose on the sea, so great that the boat was being swamped by the waves; but he was asleep. And they went and woke him up, saying, "Lord, save us! We are perishing!" And he said to them, "Why are you afraid, you of little faith?" Then he got up and rebuked the winds and the sea; and there was a dead calm. They were amazed, saying, "What sort of man is this, that even the winds and the sea obey him?"

Mt 8:23–27

" . . . but he was asleep."

When I was in my thirties and finishing my theology degree, I remember being concerned that ill health might cut my life short—that all my education might never be used. Perhaps it was a subtle anxiety that I might never make my mark on the world. Recently I've caught myself confiding to God that I wouldn't mind if he took me today or tomorrow. Life doesn't allow one to build a monument to the Lord, much less to oneself. More and more I find myself simply worshiping, surrendering in the moment, not needing to grasp it, build on it, categorize it. The moment can pass, just like every other present moment, because all that is necessary will be given to me. Someone once told me she wanted to be able to sleep as Jesus had in the boat during the storms of life. At the time it struck me as a creative understanding of that Gospel passage. Now I think I'm finally beginning to understand what she meant—absolute confidence, in the face of life or death, to remain at peace.

In life and in death I am yours, O Lord. I need nothing else but to love you forever.

62 *So be it*

Truly, O people in Zion, inhabitants of Jerusalem, you shall weep no more. He will surely be gracious to you at the sound of your cry; when he hears it, he will answer you. . . .

He will give rain for the seed with which you sow the ground, and grain, the produce of the ground, which will be rich and plenteous. . . . [T]he light of the moon will be like the light of the sun, and the light of the sun will be sevenfold, like the light of seven days, on the day when the Lord binds up the injuries of his people, and heals the wounds inflicted by his blow.

Isa 30:19, 23, 26

" . . . when the Lord binds up the injuries of his people. . . ."

I know people to whom it seems like God never speaks. Their souls are filled with a stuffy darkness. The stars have gone out. There is not a hint of the melody of God's language. They suffer because they feel God doesn't care to save them from this uncomfortable, exhausting agony.

Throughout Scripture we see individuals in this situation, peering into the darkness for a sign of God's care for them. This passage is one of those expressions of human yearning. The coming of Jesus is the fullest answer to our longing to see the light through the darkness, whatever our darkness may be. After Jesus's coming there can be no more doubt that God is with us, bending over us with care, even though we know him not.

O Silent One, Light in my darkness, Light I cannot see, Fire whose warmth I cannot feel, if I may not feel your presence, so be it. I'll remain in your dark presence unblinking. I will stand at the ready as the mystic silence of your love penetrates my heart. There will be a dawn. I know there will be dawn. There must be a dawn. But until the first streaks of light pierce the night and turn it into morning, I will live in faith that you are here, beside me. You know. You care. Whatever way you wish to be with me, so be it. I will remain with you. Amen.

63 The God who promises

For everything there is a season, and a time for every
matter under heaven:
    a time to be born, and a time to die;
    a time to plant, and a time to pluck up what is
    planted;
    a time to kill, and a time to heal;
    a time to break down, and a time to build up;
    a time to weep, and a time to laugh;
    a time to mourn, and a time to dance . . .
    a time to seek, and a time to lose . . .
    a time to keep silence, and a time to speak;
    a time to love, and a time to hate;
    a time for war, and a time for peace.

Eccl 3:1–4, 6–8

"For everything there is a season. . . ."

This passage from Ecclesiastes is famous. There is a
time for everything under the sun. God has created
an orderly world in which he has made everything suit-
able for its time. Yet the author of Ecclesiastes complains
later on in the chapter that from the beginning to the

end we cannot discover what God has done. God hasn't let us in on his secrets. Throughout salvation history God has called people to play a part in the story of his love: Noah, Abraham, Moses, Isaiah, John the Baptist, Mary, the apostle Paul. Each of these people would attest that God had something in mind when he called them, but they weren't in on the details of how it would be worked out. God does not work with strategic plans. He makes promises and leads his chosen people on winding paths that often seem to make little sense. God has also made promises to us. Faith in God's promises—and in the *God who promises*—makes the difference between seeing the situations of our life as random, hostile events or the mysterious expression of Divine Providence.

I place myself before you, Lord, as an empty canvas—paint there the story of your love for me in both bright and dark colors, with both delicate and bold strokes. Be the artist of my life.

64 Father

He was praying in a certain place, and after he had finished, one of his disciples said to him, "Lord, teach us to pray, as John taught his disciples." He said to them, "When you pray, say: Father, hallowed be your name. Your kingdom come. Give us each day our daily bread. And forgive us our sins, for we ourselves forgive everyone indebted to us. And do not bring us to the time of trial."

Lk 11:1–4

"Father. . . ."

The first word of the prayer we all learned as children, the Lord's Prayer, reminds me of the first article of the Creed: I believe in God, the *Father*. It seems to me that the "practical" parts of the Our Father—give us our daily bread, forgive us our sins, do not put us to the test—get more attention than this one most important word that stands at its head: *Father*. Jesus didn't say, *God, may your name be held holy*. He said, "Father." It is a word that indicates a relationship—a relationship of birth and of love, of life and of connection. It tells us simultaneously who God is and who we are. It signifies that God is not a force, not an idea, and not a far away regent who rules by law and punishment. God has a face, just as every father has a face. When we say "Father," we declare ourselves to be children. We exist in a filial relationship with God—safe, secure, wanted, loved, and gazed upon. We declare that we are dependent, that we too are called to love. And out of this love we desire to obey. Obedience is but a sign of our love.

May your kingdom come!

65 *The great parade*

[A] great crowd gathered around [Jesus]; and he was by the sea. Then one of the leaders of the synagogue named Jairus came and, when he saw him, fell at his feet and begged him repeatedly, "My little daughter is at the point of death. Come and lay your hands on her, so that she may be made well, and live." So he went with him. And a large crowd followed him and pressed in on him. Now there was a woman who had been suffering from hemorrhages for twelve years. . . . She had heard about Jesus, and came up behind him in the crowd and touched his cloak, for she said, "If I but touch his clothes, I will be made well."

Mk 5:21–25, 27–28

"So he went with him."

Can you imagine the parade? The joy in the air? The curiosity? The expectation? I love this passage. Jesus had been preaching and working miracles wherever he went. When Jesus arrived in this area by boat, he began to teach the crowd. A father came up and asked him to come to his home to heal his daughter. So he dropped everything and went with the distraught man. In the jostling crowd a woman tried to get a cure without anyone knowing: *I'll just touch his cloak, then I'll slip away and no one will see me.* What was Jesus like this day? What were his attitudes? Was he smiling? Was he talking to the people nearest him? Did he listen interestedly to them? Or was he grumpy? Wishing for his own personal time and space? Wishing everyone would go away and leave him alone? Too often *I'm* the grumpy one, overwhelmed by the requests of those who want help, a talk, a book, assistance with a project. I sure can't picture Jesus going about his ministry that way. This was why he came! To give his life and his love to those who needed it. He would go anywhere or do anything for someone who requested his help, surrendered their life to him, believed, repented.

Jesus, help me give myself to others as you did.

66 Breaking bread

> Now on that same day two of them were going to a village called Emmaus. . . . As they came near the village to which they were going, he walked ahead as if he were going on. But they urged him strongly, saying, "Stay with us, because it is almost evening and the day is now nearly over." So he went in to stay with them. When he was at the table with them, he took bread, blessed and broke it, and gave it to them. Then their eyes were opened, and they recognized him; and he vanished from their sight. They said to each other, "Were not our hearts burning within us while he was talking to us on the road . . . ?"
>
> Lk 24:13, 28–32

"When he was at the table with them, he took bread, blessed and broke it, and gave it to them. Then their eyes were opened. . . ."

Good Friday and Holy Saturday have always been days when I soberly remember the passion and death of the Lord, but I have not often lived the vulnerability Jesus must have experienced. The tragic terrorist attacks in New York and Washington, DC, on September

11, 2001, were an experience of this vulnerability. Any illusion of control I thought I possessed over my life, the future, or the safety of those I love was ripped away from me. That Easter was the first Easter I celebrated in the state of mind and heart of the disciples walking toward Emmaus, grieving and confused by the rapid succession of events in Jerusalem. Perhaps you have experienced this yourself. Experiences of home foreclosure, fear of losing a job, the inability to restore a loved one to health, financial disaster—all these are moments of Holy Saturday vulnerability. This delightful Gospel passage reveals to us the fidelity of God in the midst of chaotic darkness. Jesus met these two friends of his, listened to them, and broke bread with them. In this action, he healed and renewed them. We may never be able to put our worlds back together as they once were. We, like the two Emmaus disciples, can't go back to the way it was before. But in the breaking of the bread we can go forward.

Jesus, you are alive! You, the fidelity of God, are my hope and my future.

67 Simple stories

Now a man from the house of Levi went and married a Levite woman. The woman conceived and bore a son; and when she saw that he was a fine baby, she hid him three months. When she could hide him no longer she got a papyrus basket for him, and plastered it with bitumen and pitch; she put the child in it and placed it among the reeds on the bank of the river. His sister stood at a distance, to see what would happen to him . . . [Pharaoh's daughter] took him as her son. She named him Moses, "because," she said, "I drew him out of the water."

Ex 2:1–4, 10

" . . . she hid him three months."

Under the shadow of the Egyptian government's crushing power and Pharaoh's oppression of the Hebrew people, one small Levite family fell in love with their baby boy and decided to hide him from the authorities. Such a simple story, but for those of us who are sometimes overwhelmed by the power of government, the tragedy of war, and the news of famine and oppression, the story of Moses is a paradigm. God is here. God is present and active in our world. God does mighty things through small, everyday actions. God doesn't need attention, troops, or announcements. God works in little ways, ways so hidden that we barely notice them. In fact, we can hardly believe that the small things of our own lives are part of the glorious drama of salvation. I'm sure Moses's mother was glad that she had saved the life of her son. There was no way for her to know, however, that she had saved the one who would set her people free. Such a simple story—as simple as our own. Often, we too have no idea of the full weight of the simple things we do.

Mighty God, Guardian of our lives, use the simple things I do to accomplish the mystery of your plan of love and salvation.

68 Getting God's attention

"Ask and it will be given to you; seek and you will find;
knock and the door will be opened to you. For everyone who asks, receives; and the one who seeks, finds;
and to the one who knocks, the door will be opened.
Which one of you would hand his son a stone when he
asks for a loaf of bread, or a snake when he asks for a
fish? If you then, who are wicked, know how to give
good gifts to your children, how much more will your
heavenly Father give good things to those who ask
him."

Mt 7:7–11 (NABRE)

"Ask and it will be given to you; seek and you will find. . . ."

Retreats, holy hours, novenas, prayer chains. . . . All
of these in some way hearken back to this promise
of Jesus: *Ask, seek, knock, and what you desire will be yours.*
Whether we are asking for material or spiritual blessings
for others or for ourselves, this image of prayer reminds

us of children attempting to get God's attention. Indeed, the parental image of God is suggested by Jesus himself, "Which one of you would hand his son a stone?" One day God said to me, *Everything you need I've already given you*. These seven words flipped my spiritual life on its head! God was saying that the present moment contains everything I need. To the three activities of asking, seeking, and knocking, therefore, there now correspond the three activities of thanking, receiving, and enjoying. God calls us *also* to be perfectly happy with what we have received. After all, a good parent will give more to a child who appreciates what he or she has been given.

Father of Jesus and my Father, I thank you for all that has been in my life, for all that is, and for all that will be.

69 *Lay aside immaturity*

Wisdom has built her house,
    she has hewn her seven pillars.
She has slaughtered her animals, she has mixed her wine,
    she has also set her table.
She has sent out her servant-girls, she calls
    from the highest places in the town,
"You that are simple, turn in here!"
    To those without sense she says,
"Come, eat of my bread
    and drink of the wine I have mixed.
Lay aside immaturity, and live,
    and walk in the way of insight."

Prov 9:1–6

"Wisdom has built her house. . . ."

I am writing this on an airplane while watching *Charlie and the Chocolate Factory*. It is a wonderful backdrop to this passage from the book of Proverbs. "You that are simple, turn in here! . . . Lay aside immaturity." Each of the characters becomes the victim of their foolishness or fears, while Charlie's simplicity and wisdom bring reconciliation and healing to Willy Wonka, and a better life to Charlie's beloved family. This selection from the treasure of God's wisdom shows us how to live our lives in this simplicity: as intelligent and not like senseless people (cf. Jer 4:22). Seek the Lord, listen to him, be teachable, leave aside evil and deceit, seek peace, recognize God's will. In this way, filled with the Spirit, we will give thanks to the Father and live and mature in Christ by receiving his Body and Blood in the Eucharist.

Lord, in the chaotic confusion of life that can overwhelm me at times, guide me in the ways of perception that I may attain eternal life.

70 Come, Lord Jesus

John to the seven churches that are in Asia: Grace to you and peace from him who is and who was and who is to come, and from the seven spirits who are before his throne, and from Jesus Christ, the faithful witness, the firstborn of the dead, and the ruler of the kings of the earth. To him who loves us and freed us from our sins by his blood, and made us to be a kingdom, priests serving his God and Father, to him be glory and dominion forever and ever. Amen. "I am the Alpha and the Omega," says the Lord God, who is and who was and who is to come, the Almighty.

Rev 1:4–6, 8

" . . . to him be glory and dominion forever and ever."

The book of Revelation is a comforting guide to Christians of every age. John never sugarcoats the fact that we must contend with the powers of the world we live in. We deal with the values of a society often far from Christian in its orientation, the problems of a complex and confusing technological era suffering from the fact that what we can do far outstrips our ethical reflection. We will contend with the principalities of the world until the close of history. Jesus Christ, the faithful witness, sees everything. Let this passage give you a bit of confidence. Let it pierce the darkness you may see around you with a shaft of light falling from the open door of eternity. Remember, however, that the beginning of the Book of Revelation does not castigate the rulers of Babylon and the emperors of Rome. Instead it speaks quite strongly to the Christians in the seven churches in Asia. This is a good corrective to our perceptions that the problem is all "out there" in the darkness. The Book of Revelation calls us to be more of who we already are, to give the Lord glory and dominion in our lives, to let him be the Alpha and the Omega of our personal history.

Come, Lord Jesus, come, now, here. Come into my heart. Come into the world. Come transform our history. Come, Lord Jesus, come!

71 *Nothing is arbitrary*

The Lord said to Abram, after Lot had separated from him, "Raise your eyes now, and look from the place where you are, northward and southward and eastward and westward; for all the land that you see I will give to you and to your offspring forever. I will make your offspring like the dust of the earth; so that if one can count the dust of the earth, your offspring also can be counted. Rise up, walk through the length and the breadth of the land, for I will give it to you." So Abram moved his tent, and came and settled by the oaks of Mamre, which are at Hebron; and there he built an altar to the Lord.

Gen 13:14–18

" . . . all the land that you see
I will give to you and to your offspring forever."

My life can seem arbitrary sometimes. "We need a person with a degree in this role, will you accept a transfer?" "We don't understand what you are doing, could you develop something different?" "This is Plan B because Plan A didn't work out. We need you to move to another city." Sound familiar? The wonderful message of this passage from Genesis is that there is *nothing* arbitrary with God. Abraham gave Lot first pick, and, as could be expected, Lot took the best for himself. Abraham got Plan B. God, however, reaffirmed that he had a plan for Abraham's life. His life had a goal, a purpose, a meaning. That meaning was sheer gift. He didn't have to seize it like Lot who was calculating how to get the best for himself. My life—and yours—is also sheer gift. Despite the seeming arbitrariness, reversals, and frustrations, we are on a journey and the journey has a goal. It doesn't wind aimlessly around only to hit a dead-end. The destination is clear, and nothing will prevent us from reaching it as long as we, like Abraham, listen to God, obey his word, and worship him.

I am listening, trying to listen to you, the One who gives true meaning to my life. When I seem to be running in circles or to have hit a dead-end, let me hear your voice.

72 My Father's hands

"I revealed your name to those whom you gave me out of the world. They belonged to you, and you gave them to me, and they have kept your word. Now they know that everything you gave me is from you, because the words you gave to me I have given to them, and they accepted them and truly understood that I came from you, and they have believed that you sent me. I pray for them. I do not pray for the world but for the ones you have given me, because they are yours, and everything of mine is yours and everything of yours is mine, and I have been glorified in them."

Jn 17:6–10 (NABRE)

" . . . they are yours, and everything of mine is yours and everything of yours is mine. . . ."

When people speak with me about death—their own impending death, whether they perceive it to be proximate or remote—their voice conveys trepidation, uncertainty, and fear. In this Gospel passage, which is from Jesus's last discourse, Jesus faces his own death with serenity. Serenity is the result of knowing that you cannot control the world around you or the time and manner of your death, but that you can nonetheless respond to and embrace what life—and death—brings you. Jesus's life and his death were by this time already in the hands of others. He knew that through these hands he was also, always and forever, in the hands of his Father. Jesus makes it clear that we too are, always and forever, in the hands of the Father. We belong to the Father, consecrated and chosen from the beginning of the world. We belong to the Son whose passionate love led him to throw himself into our midst and lift us to everything God had dreamt for us to have and to be. Although it is natural to tremble before the uncertainty of death, we can find hope in the reliability of Love who holds us and saves us forever.

Our Father, who art in heaven, hallowed—yes, forever hallowed—be thy name.

73 A difficult choice made in the dark

The people spoke against God and against Moses, "Why have you brought us up out of Egypt to die in the wilderness? For there is no food and no water, and we detest this miserable food." Then the LORD sent poisonous serpents among the people, and they bit the people, so that many Israelites died. The people came to Moses and said, "We have sinned by speaking against the LORD and against you; pray to the LORD to take away the serpents from us." So Moses prayed for the people. And the LORD said to Moses, "Make a poisonous serpent, and set it on a pole; and everyone who is bitten shall look at it and live."

Num 21:5–8

" . . . we detest this miserable food."

I wonder what would have happened if instead of complaining, the people had sought to see how God was acting *for* them in their frustrating desert experience. In the last seven chapters of Numbers, God has replied five times to their complaints. In none of those times does God sympathize with their complaint. Instead, God said of those who muttered against him, "[They] have seen my glory and the signs that I did in Egypt and in the wilderness, and yet have tested me . . ." (Num 14:22). These words show us that the opposite of muttering is not resignation (grin and bear it), but covenant relationship. God has also shown *us* his glory, working marvels for us. Instead of muttering complaints, therefore, which can come seemingly unbidden to our minds, we need to turn to our hearts. The heart asks questions. The heart seeks to understand and struggles to remain in relationship. When we encounter the vicissitudes that beset us on our desert pilgrimage to the Father, the devil wants nothing more than the grumblings that lead to distrust and rejection. Faith in God being with us and for us—a difficult choice always made in the dark—leads us to trust, acceptance, and peace.

Lord, instead of being disgusted with a situation, I will ask simply, *Lord, what is going on here? Where are you? Show me your face, and I shall be saved.*

74 Discovering Love

"[I]n all these things we are more than conquerors through him who loved us. For I am convinced that neither death, nor life, nor angels, nor rulers, nor things present, nor things to come, nor powers, nor height, nor depth, nor anything else in all creation, will be able to separate us from the love of God in Christ Jesus our Lord."

Rom 8:37–39

"For I am convinced. . . ."

Sometimes it seems that we need to move mountains to get ourselves to believe in God's love for us. I remember as a novice telling a venerable old superior that I thought I didn't believe God loved me. "My dear," she responded, "this is a truth of faith! You must believe it." After that I certainly didn't bring up the topic again! But in my heart, I wanted so much the reassurance of knowing God's love for me. I wished there was some surefire method a person could follow to feel God's love. *Fortunately* there isn't. For if we could manipulate our feelings of God's presence so easily, it certainly wouldn't be God's love that we were experiencing. Whether we feel God's love or not, the fact is we *are* loved by God. Without that love we wouldn't exist, for we are completely dependent on God. While there is no method, there is a *secret* to discovering God's love. Divine love begins with desire and grows with faith.

Lord, show me your face. Pour into my soul all the love that you are. Whether I feel your love or not, I shall believe your love surrounds and holds me in existence. Nothing will shake this certainty.

75 *A truly creative act*

In the sixth month the angel Gabriel was sent by God
to a town in Galilee called Nazareth, to a virgin engaged
to a man whose name was Joseph, of the house of
David. The virgin's name was Mary. And he came to
her and said, "Greetings, favored one! The Lord is with
you." But she was much perplexed by his words and
pondered what sort of greeting this might be. The
angel said to her, "Do not be afraid, Mary, for you have
found favor with God. And now, you will conceive in
your womb and bear a son, and you will name him
Jesus. . . ." Then Mary said, "Here am I, the servant of
the Lord; let it be with me according to your word."

Lk 1:26–31, 38

" . . . let it be with me according to your word."

Obedience is a creative activity. Mary's words to the
angel, "Let it be with me according to your word,"
directly reflect the words of God the Creator, "Let it be"
(cf. Gen 1:3). Certainly the Creator acted in power as he
called into being galaxies and sky, stars and grass,

mountains and chipmunks, tigers and elephants, and finally, man and woman. It is easy to make the mistake that to take part in creative activity we need to have the unhindered freedom to call projects into being, to do as we please, to create something that will last and bear our name into the future, to develop ourselves and command others. It is Mary, however, who shows us the authentic human way of participating in God's creative activity: "Let it be done to me." Obedience, surrender, receptivity, and the desire to play our part in salvation history, the part written just for us—these are truly creative acts, because we allow God to create in us and through us for others. We hand over to God, as Mary did, our bodies, minds, and wills, our hopes and dreams, our futures, sufferings, and successes.

Lord, by participating in your creative act, I am pulled out of the small future I've dreamt for myself and emerge onto the stage of salvation history which reaches far into the future and has no end. Let it be done to me.

76 *Sustained by intimacy*

Jesus, knowing that the Father had given all things into his hands, and that he had come from God and was going to God, got up from the table, took off his outer robe, and tied a towel around himself. Then he poured water into a basin and began to wash the disciples' feet and to wipe them with the towel that was tied around him.

Jn 13:3–5

" . . . [Jesus] began to wash the disciples' feet. . . ."

With these words John begins his account of what we have come to call the Last Supper. This particular account of the final meal before Jesus's death has become very meaningful to me. First of all, Jesus had a full schedule of ministry and knew his life was in danger. In the midst of all this Jesus stopped and called his followers together for a meal. He sought to comfort them and to derive support from the intimacy of the Passover meal. It wasn't a perfunctory following of the instructions for the Passover meal. Instead it began with a disconcerting act of humble hospitality. In his humanity, not knowing the future, was Jesus wondering if this was the only time he would be able to wash the feet of the men who had come to mean so much to him? If so, with what attention and tenderness he must have knelt before them. He spoke to them individually, as we see in his conversations with Peter and later with Thomas. Jesus— the giver of hospitality—has become my mentor. How can I provide a kind and welcoming invitation to others to relax, to be refreshed, to let themselves be cared for, to pause for times of intimacy and deep reflection and feeling?

Jesus, help me stop worrying about my schedule so that I can create places of intimacy and hospitality where others may rest and we may be renewed together.

77 *The path of holiness*

Although you have not seen him, you love him; and even though you do not see him now, you believe in him and rejoice with an indescribable and glorious joy, for you are receiving the outcome of your faith, the salvation of your souls. . . . Therefore prepare your minds for action; discipline yourselves; set all your hope on the grace that Jesus Christ will bring you when he is revealed. Like obedient children, do not be conformed to the desires that you formerly had in ignorance. Instead, as he who called you is holy, be holy yourselves in all your conduct; for it is written, "You shall be holy, for I am holy."

1 Pet 1:8–9, 13–16

" . . . *be holy. . . .*"

I remember many years ago reading about a business executive from the United States who spent her vacation working in a home she had founded for orphans in a third world country. For her, vacation was a chance to revitalize her life by doing what she really wanted to do:

help others. This was her path of holiness. I know a mother whose two children are challenged in different ways. One has Down's syndrome and the other is waiting for a lung transplant. This is her path of holiness. I have another friend whose wife left him. He makes every decision for the good of their three little girls. In a simple way his loneliness is transformed into solitude with a rarely found contemplative depth. This is his path of holiness. We each walk our own paths of holiness, because *although we have not seen Jesus, we love him. Even though we do not see him now, we believe in him and follow him, hoping in a future of indescribable and glorious joy.*

Pluck me, Lord, out of ease and comfort. Take me into the depths where you give yourself to those who love you. Let me weather the storm in peace. Give me a ready ear, an open heart, a humble mind, and a firm will. I surrender all to you. Amen.

78 *The wine of sorrow*

Then the LORD answered Job out of the whirlwind:
 " . . . I will question you, and you shall declare to me.
"Where were you when I laid the foundation of the earth?
 Tell me, if you have understanding. . . ."
Then Job answered the LORD:
 "I know that you can do all things,
  and that no purpose of yours can be thwarted. . . .
Therefore I have uttered what I did not understand,
 things too wonderful for me, which I did not
    know. . . .
I had heard of you by the hearing of the ear,
 but now my eye sees you;
therefore I despise myself,
 and repent in dust and ashes."

                              Job 38:1, 3–4; 42:1–2, 3b, 5–6

" . . . but now my eye sees you. . . ."

None of us, after we reach a certain age, can look
into the mirror without remembering the dark
wine of sorrow in our lives. Disillusionment, anger, frustration, and bitterness may have filled our thoughts and

hearts as we struggled through these days, weeks, and years of pain. Looking back, was there any meaning to it all? Have you ever asked God, *why?* Has God answered you? Are you still angry? Do you feel cheated in life? Has there been a resolution to the pain? Has it changed you, molded your character, made you more understanding of others, more gentle, more kind? This passage from the book of Job shows us some remarkable things about God. First, God holds us in such esteem that he speaks to us directly about our pain. Second, not one tiny thing escapes God's attention. Like the most observant mother, God knows every detail of what happens to each of us. Third, our complaints about what happens to us are like the prattling of a child. We forget that in some mysterious fashion, nothing can thwart the purposes of God. Lastly, it is often only in the struggle initiated through suffering that we come to the point of truly seeing God.

Lord, I long to hear your voice. Come into the temple of my heart that I may receive you, worship you, be taught by you.

79 Beginning again

I will now allure her,
  and bring her into the wilderness,
  and speak tenderly to her. . . .
There she shall respond as in the days of her youth,
  as at the time when she came out of the land of
    Egypt.
On that day, says the LORD, you will call me, "My husband," and no longer will you call me, "My Baal." For I
will remove the names of the Baals from her mouth,
and they shall be mentioned by name no more. . . . And
I will take you for my wife forever; I will take you for
my wife in righteousness and in justice, in steadfast
love, and in mercy. I will take you for my wife in faith-
fulness; and you shall know the LORD.

                                         Hos 2:14–17, 19–20

"I will take you for my wife forever. . . ."

Since over thirty years ago when I discovered this passage, I have come back to the wonderful book of
Hosea again and again. This book describes God's relationship with his Chosen People as a marriage in which

the wife has committed adultery. The husband takes her back again and again, only to have her leave him in search of other lovers. The point of the book of Hosea is that Israel, the bride of God, is accused of adultery because she has followed idols and relied on foreign nations and gods for protection. Punishment was sure to come, a punishment meant to save them. Under no circumstances could Israel be considered a "virgin"; she is rather an unfaithful wife. However, God calls out to Israel to woo her as a man tries to win over a woman to be his bride. He has forgotten her adulterous past—he promises to abolish it—and is ready to begin again. In his new marriage with Israel he will make her a new creature. The story of Israel is the story of God's relationship with each of us.

In an instant, O God, you can abolish my past, my wayward ways, choices that led me down paths far from you. In an instant you can bring me back to you. You can throw the past away, never to be brought up again. We can begin again, Lord. You and I. Amen.

80 *How great is God's love*

See what love the Father has bestowed on us that we may be called the children of God. Yet so we are. The reason the world does not know us is that it did not know him. Beloved, we are God's children now; what we shall be has not yet been revealed. We do know that when it is revealed we shall be like him, for we shall see him as he is. Everyone who has this hope based on him makes himself pure, as he is pure.

1 Jn 3:1–3 (NABRE)

" . . . we shall be like him. . . ."

Jesus's last will and testament was that his disciples would see and *share* in the glory that he has with the Father. Thus, this seeing becomes *participation*. We watch movies about Jesus or read the Scriptures. Often we feel "on the outside looking in." In reality, though, we have been loved with an extravagant, undeserved love and have been granted a share in God's life through the Holy Spirit who has been poured into our hearts. It is the Spirit within us who is the guarantee that our participation in the life of God will not end in disgrace. God himself has given us the promise and is quickening within us the divine life to come. God himself will keep his promise in us. This is a consolation for all those who mourn and worry about their loved ones who have left the practice of their faith or who no longer believe in God. Remind God of his promises to us, of the first fruits of salvation already sown in our lives at our Baptism through the Spirit's gift. We are called to abide in the Spirit's love within us, and God will chase after the person who runs from his love.

In your hands, my God, I place all those who flee from you. Let their journey ultimately end up in your arms.

PART V

Lord, I Will Follow You Wherever You Go

81 *The free follower of Providence*

[S]omeone said to him, "I will follow you wherever you go." And Jesus said to him, "Foxes have holes, and birds of the air have nests; but the Son of Man has nowhere to lay his head." To another he said, "Follow me." But he said, "Lord, first let me go and bury my father." But Jesus said to him, "Let the dead bury their own dead; but as for you, go and proclaim the kingdom of God." Another said, "I will follow you, Lord; but let me first say farewell to those at my home." Jesus said to him, "No one who puts a hand to the plow and looks back is fit for the kingdom of God."

Lk 9:57–62

"I will follow you wherever you go."

The one who spoke these words had it all wrong. We also, too often, have it all wrong. Children of rationalism, we think that it is *we* who decide to follow, we who understand, we who choose. We submit the mystery to our intellectual mastery. Jesus instead replied that mastery has no place in the mystery of salvation.

"The Son of Man has nowhere to lay his head." Jesus had no control even over where he would sleep each night. He was the free follower of the Providence that takes care of sparrows and dresses the fields with flowers. Jesus was complete receptivity. Jesus was total obedience. In a world that submits everything to its own criteria of importance and worth, Jesus had no property, security, or credentials. He remained the everlasting child of the Father and said that those who follow him must also become children—small, trusting, having no need to build themselves up or show themselves off. St. Thérèse understood this childhood, writing in her *Story of a Soul*, "[Lord,] for me to love you as you love me, I would have to borrow your own love. . . . I cannot conceive a greater immensity of love than the one which it has pleased you to give me freely, *without any merit on my part*."

Lord, make of me, work through me, give to me, only and always what *you* desire.

82 *Declaring our commitment*

Now when Jesus came into the district of Caesarea Philippi, he asked his disciples, "Who do people say that the Son of Man is?" And they said, "Some say John the Baptist, but others Elijah, and still others Jeremiah or one of the prophets." He said to them, "But who do you say that I am?" Simon Peter answered, "You are the Messiah, the Son of the living God."

Mt 16:13–16

"But who do you say that I am?"

This was a major turning point. The Twelve had been following the Teacher. They had witnessed miracles, heard him teach, watched him pray. But now, they had to step out of the shadows and bring into sharp focus who Jesus was for them. "Who do you say that I am?" Upon their answers rested a level of commitment. After Peter's answer he could no longer go back to the happy early days of Jesus's ministry with the crowds following him in astonished praise. No. Now Jesus spoke of his passion, of the commitment demanded of anyone who wishes to share in his life. For us also, God is often in the background of our lives. Situations arise when we have to declare our level of commitment to the Lord. From that point forward he becomes central to our lives, not immediately, but in a gradual daily re-choosing of his way.

Master, you are everything for me. I want to be entirely for you. May I look into your eyes and promise you my love till my last breath.

83 *God is bursting into the world*

Then Jesus called the twelve together and gave them power and authority over all demons and to cure diseases, and he sent them out to proclaim the kingdom of God and to heal. He said to them, "Take nothing for your journey, no staff, nor bag, nor bread, nor money—not even an extra tunic. Whatever house you enter, stay there, and leave from there. Wherever they do not welcome you, as you are leaving that town shake the dust off your feet as a testimony against them."

Lk 9:1–5

" . . . [Jesus] sent them out to proclaim the kingdom of God. . . ."

Jesus sent the apostles out to proclaim the kingdom of God—an announcement that God is bursting into the world in the person of Jesus Christ. With this vision of reality we become grounded in our truest self: we are citizens of God's kingdom. Without this vision of reality, we become knocked off-course by every stress, obstacle, or dismay we encounter. This faith is the light and power that nourishes our thoughts and builds true self-esteem. It gives us the confidence to believe in the sustaining love of God for us. I don't know about you, but it is so easy for me to read about faith, and at the same time so difficult to take responsibility for the way I think. My thoughts flitter here and there, getting lost in every anxiety and distortion, leading me far away from the joy of living in the kingdom of God. I shrink before the onslaught of disturbing news, fearing that negativity and not love may be the center of the universe. My thoughts become traps, torn away from what alone can heal me: the announcement that *God is here*.

Jesus, steady my mind that I may look into each situation with the security of knowing myself a child of the Father, at home in your Kingdom. Amen.

84 Someone is waiting for your story

They went to Capernaum; and when the sabbath came, he entered the synagogue and taught. They were astounded at his teaching, for he taught them as one having authority, and not as the scribes. . . . They were all amazed, and they kept on asking one another, "What is this? A new teaching—with authority! He commands even the unclean spirits, and they obey him." At once his fame began to spread throughout the surrounding region of Galilee.

Mk 1:21–22, 27–28

"At once his fame began to spread throughout the surrounding region of Galilee."

Ah! The "grapevine" at its best. Without e-mail, phones, or UPS, without Twitter, YouTube, or Facebook, the word got out. *Have you heard the latest? There is a new teacher in town. No one told you? You should hear how he speaks. My heart was moved like never before. And as if that wasn't enough, he even healed someone with an unclean spirit, right there in the synagogue! Maybe he can cure your mother!* With all the means of communication we have, the grapevine is still the most personal way to catch up on the latest. What runs through our grapevines? Gossip, scandal, the latest news items? What would happen if we, like these ancient Galilean settlers, filled our grapevines and rumor mills with what God has done for us? Two thousand years ago the rumor mill got crowds to come out and listen to Jesus. Curiosity, interest, and desire drew them. They discovered that these rumors were actually true. The stories on the grapevine caused people to hope, to trust, to long for peace, to desire to change. These little messages created a movement. Do you have an experience of God's love you could share? Someone might just be waiting for your story!

Lord, we need you now. How can I speak of you so that others will want to listen? What means do I have at my fingertips that will help me share your love? Are you calling me to this?

85 *God will do it himself*

Now may our God and Father himself and our Lord
Jesus direct our way to you. And may the Lord make
you increase and abound in love for one another and
for all, just as we abound in love for you. And may he
so strengthen your hearts in holiness that you may be
blameless before our God and Father at the coming of
our Lord Jesus with all his saints.

1 Thess 3:11–13

"And may the Lord make you increase and abound in love. . . ."

Contrary to what you've been told, *you* can't do it.
You can't live a moral life. You can't obey God's
law. As St. Augustine said, it is not in our power to live as
God desires. So give up trying and *start praying*. Paul
prayed for his beloved Christians in Thessalonica: "And
may *the Lord* make you increase and abound in love . . .
may *he* so strengthen your hearts in holiness that you
may be blameless before our God and Father" (emphasis
added). Perhaps that is why Paul was so full of gratitude.

He knew that what he couldn't do himself, God wanted to give him. Paul needed to pray, ponder, love, hope, and live in love with Jesus who had sought him out. If he continuously turned himself over to God's power, God would transform him in that power into all God desired. There is a prayer I once found that would make us fly on the path of holiness: "Lord, accomplish in me, yourself, all that you desire of me."

Lord, *I* can't do it. Most of the time I forget this, but whether I remember it or not, the fact is that you want to do in me what I can't do. Lord, accomplish in me, yourself, all that you desire of me.

86 *Becoming a neighbor*

But wanting to justify himself, he asked Jesus, "And who is my neighbor?" Jesus replied, "A man was going down from Jerusalem to Jericho, and fell into the hands of robbers. . . . Now by chance a priest was going down that road; and when he saw him, he passed by on the other side. So likewise a Levite, when he came to the place and saw him, passed by on the other side. But a Samaritan while traveling came near him; and when he saw him, he was moved with pity. . . . Which of these three, do you think, was a neighbor to the man who fell into the hands of the robbers?" He said, "The one who showed him mercy."

Lk 10:29–33, 36–37

"Which of these three . . . was a neighbor?"

If you are like me, I begin the day with too many things to do, meetings back to back, and a list of people I don't want to run into because I know they'll upset my schedule. Like the man who asked Jesus, *So, who is my neighbor,* I too want to narrowly define neighbor, squeezing it into the few people and interruptions I can reasonably deal with. Jesus, however, is not interested in that question. In fact, he doesn't even answer it. After his tale of the man beaten and left for dead on the side of the road, Jesus asks a different question: *In this story, who has* been *the neighbor?* It is not a question of selecting those to whom I will dole out a few moments of compassion during the day. It is a matter of realizing that I need to become the neighbor who, despite inconvenience, expense, and deadlines not met, drops everything to attend to another's need. Indeed, it is precisely on this that my final judgment will be based: feeding the hungry, visiting the imprisoned, clothing the naked.

Lord, I beg you, let me be a neighbor to someone today.

87 We are Christ's body

When it was evening on that day, the first day of the week, and the doors of the house where the disciples had met were locked for fear of the Jews, Jesus came and stood among them and said, "Peace be with you." After he said this, he showed them his hands and his side. Then the disciples rejoiced when they saw the Lord. Jesus said to them again, "Peace be with you. As the Father has sent me, so I send you." When he had said this, he breathed on them and said to them, "Receive the Holy Spirit. If you forgive the sins of any, they are forgiven them; if you retain the sins of any, they are retained."

Jn 20:19–23

"As the Father has sent me, so I send you."

Jesus knew what it was to be sent. He—completely and eagerly obedient—was sent to live among us. He healed, loved, and blessed us. He relaxed in our company. He spent his days preaching and forgiving and teaching us to pray. He faced the utter finality of the darkness of death. Now he was sending his disciples—once fragile and afraid, now boldly transformed—to continue his work. Our deepest meaning, our essence as Church is this belonging to Christ who has named us friends, it is this being sent into the world as his body, this having been brought into existence by the Eucharist and transformed by the fire of the Spirit.

Lord, in all the struggles your Church suffers today, help us remember we are more than a group of self-appointed people who have decided to follow you. We are the body of Christ. We have been chosen and sent, loved and forgiven by you to whom we belong forever. Amen.

88 *It isn't crazy*

Then he went home; and the crowd came together again, so that they could not even eat. When his family heard it, they went out to restrain him, for people were saying, "He has gone out of his mind."

Mk 3:19–21

"He has gone out of his mind."

This is a perplexing Gospel passage. Why did Jesus's relatives think he was crazy? Here he was: an amazing healer, teacher, and prophet surrounded by disciples and sought after by crowds. Was it because he was so busy that he seemed to reserve no time for himself? Or was he attracting too much attention and putting himself or them at risk? Or was it perhaps the same thing that makes *us* wonder if Jesus is crazy? Love your enemies (cf. Mt 5:44). . . . Let anyone among you who is without sin be the first to throw a stone (cf. Jn 8:7). . . . Moses allowed you to write a bill of divorce, but it was not that way from the beginning (cf. Mk 10:4–5). . . . Take up your cross (cf. Lk 9:23). . . . You cannot serve God and wealth (cf. Mt 6:24). . . . The first will be last (cf. Mt 20:16). . . . Doesn't Jesus understand how utterly impossible these things sound? Has *he* felt human passions and been hurt at a brother's hands? We forget he has. Jesus knows that what he asks *sounds* crazy, because we can't do it alone. Only if we are grafted onto Jesus the living Vine will we be able to bear the living fruit he is talking about.

I'm a little shamefaced, Jesus. I have not always lived according to these seemingly crazy commands of yours. Give me today some time apart to shape my priorities and values according to your heart.

89 *Drawn to new depths*

> "And now, Lord . . . grant to your servants to speak your word with all boldness, while you stretch out your hand to heal, and signs and wonders are performed through the name of your holy servant Jesus." When they had prayed, the place in which they were gathered together was shaken; and they were all filled with the Holy Spirit and spoke the word of God with boldness.
>
> Acts 4:29–31

> *"When they had prayed, the place*
> *in which they were gathered together was shaken;*
> *and they were all filled with the Holy Spirit. . . ."*

The manifestation of power accompanying the prayers and ministry of the apostles as recorded in the Acts of the Apostles should cause us to wake up to the power of God that breaks upon us when we worship as a community and minister in God's name. Annie Dillard says in her book *Holy the Firm* that we Christians are too unaware of, almost insensible to, the power of the name we invoke. If we truly understood the liturgy we celebrate, the church buildings would rock. No more would we walk into the church with such low expectations that nothing much different from the week before could possibly happen. In reality, God might just draw us out to new depths. God might take us to a place from which we could never return. We do not wait today for the *buildings* where we worship to shake with the power of God. Instead, the power expressed in the Acts of the Apostles is about the shaking of our hearts. The over-turning of our worlds of meaning. The upsurge of new sources of life and vitality. The overwhelming power of the presence of the Spirit of Jesus. May the place in my life from which I pray shake with the power of God that breaks upon me.

Break open, Lord, our slumbering stony hearts and shape for yourself a new people!

90 *The world cries out*

The one who comes from above is above all; the one who is of the earth belongs to the earth and speaks about earthly things. The one who comes from heaven is above all. He testifies to what he has seen and heard, yet no one accepts his testimony. Whoever has accepted his testimony has certified this, that God is true. He whom God has sent speaks the words of God, for he gives the Spirit without measure. The Father loves the Son and has placed all things in his hands. Whoever believes in the Son has eternal life; whoever disobeys the Son will not see life, but must endure God's wrath.

Jn 3:31–36

> *"He testifies to what he has seen and heard,*
> *yet no one accepts his testimony."*

In this passage we eavesdrop on a conversation between Nicodemus and Jesus about the witness of belief in the midst of the world. People enter into this dialogue between faith and culture in three different ways. Some suffer from a failure of nerve and build a fence around the faith, protecting it lest the culture contaminate it. Others make the faith over in the image of the culture, baptizing cultural expressions in the name of the Gospel. The third group, however, has enough trust in faith to get involved in the culture without identifying with it. They offer a particular kind of resistance and challenge to the culture. "And we are witnesses to these things, and so is the Holy Spirit whom God has given to those who obey him" (Acts 5:32). "Whoever believes in the Son has eternal life." The world needs witnesses. It cries out despite itself for people of courage, willing to confront it with "the one who comes from heaven." For it somehow knows that in the end, only life open to the eternal can be called life at all.

May I open my heart wide to the world, inviting all to come to the feast the Savior sets. May all find in me consolation, compassionate guidance, and healing love.

91 Sabbath space

At that time Jesus went through the grainfields on the sabbath; his disciples were hungry, and they began to pluck heads of grain and to eat. When the Pharisees saw it, they said to him, "Look, your disciples are doing what is not lawful to do on the sabbath." He said to them, "Have you not read what David did when he and his companions were hungry? He entered the house of God and ate the bread of the Presence, which it was not lawful for him or his companions to eat. . . . But if you had known what this means, 'I desire mercy and not sacrifice,' you would not have condemned the guiltless. For the Son of Man is lord of the sabbath."

Mt 12:1–4, 7–8

"Look, your disciples are doing
what is not lawful to do on the sabbath."

The basic law to keep holy the Sabbath was established in order for people to remember and reflect on their special covenant relationship with God who had delivered them from slavery and given them rest. The Sabbath precept, which prepares for the Sunday of the new and eternal covenant, is an indelible expression of our relationship with God. Sunday has been kept sacred by the Church because it commemorates the day of the Lord's resurrection. For centuries this day was also preserved from work because human dignity requires appropriate rest and leisure. The true meaning of work can only appear when it is alternated with rest. For some of us, the harried pace of life has blurred Sunday into any other day of the week, except that people go to church. Why not establish some other Sunday ritual that expresses the joy of your relationship with God? It could be a walk, a time of prayer, family time together, a special meal, a slowed down pace after supper, an hour without the TV being on. For your own sake, carve out some Sabbath space for you and God. The length of time doesn't matter as much as your desire to honor the Lord's covenant with us and his mercy in setting us free and giving us rest.

My Lord, how my heart longs for spaces of Sabbath rest. Help me cherish these sacred moments of reverent rest with you.

92 *A tremendous adventure*

"'Those who try to make their life secure will lose it, but those who lose their life will keep it. I tell you, on that night there will be two in one bed; one will be taken and the other left. There will be two women grinding meal together; one will be taken and the other left.'"

Lk 17:33–35

" . . . one will be taken and the other left."

This Gospel passage could be a rather grim read—destruction, sin, fire and brimstone, losing life, a sudden visitation of the Son of Man that separates one from another. . . . Every passage of Scripture, however, needs to be seen in the light of the rest of the sacred word. The readings at a recent funeral of one of our sisters could be read as a foil to this Gospel passage: "The voice of my beloved! Look, he comes. . . . My beloved speaks and says to me: 'Arise, my love, my fair one, and come away. . .'" (Song 2:8ff.). And ". . . a woman came with an alabaster jar of very costly ointment of nard, and she broke open the jar and poured the ointment on his head" (Mk 14:3ff.). These readings, read side by side with this Gospel passage, point out that Christianity, although lived out within the Christian community, is an almost terrifying personal responsibility as well as a tremendous adventure of life and love. By ourselves we cannot live a God-like life. We lose our life, which Jesus calls his followers to do, so that we can be brought back to life by God, a life that is as fragrant as an expensive perfume and as promising as newly-wedded love.

Take my life, Lord, and use it. Draw me and I will run after you.

93 *Bring them to Jesus*

When they came to the crowd, a man came to him, knelt before him, and said, "Lord, have mercy on my son, for he is an epileptic and he suffers terribly; he often falls into the fire and often into the water. And I brought him to your disciples, but they could not cure him." Jesus answered, "You faithless and perverse generation, how much longer must I be with you? How much longer must I put up with you? Bring him here to me." And Jesus rebuked the demon, and it came out of him, and the boy was cured instantly.

Mt 17:14–18

"And I brought him to your disciples, but they could not cure him."

Sometimes I find myself acting like these disciples. Just as this father brings his epileptic son to the disciples of Jesus to be healed, friends might bring me their struggles or a stranger might ask for prayers. When this happens, I feel responsible for conjuring up the miracle that will save the situation or heal the broken heart. I can imagine the disciples in Jesus's absence trying to figure out what to do, maybe trying a few things they had seen their Master do. But when Jesus arrives on the scene the father runs and throws himself at his feet with the utmost dependence and confidence. He had brought his boy to the disciples only because he believed they would bring him to Jesus, not try to figure out some makeshift human solution of their own. How embarrassed I feel before Jesus, when I realize I have tried to create miracles on my own. People really want to be brought to Jesus.

Lord, help me become, in some mysterious way, a pipeline for you to exercise your divine activity today.

94 What is the kingdom of God like?

He said therefore, "What is the kingdom of God like? And to what should I compare it? It is like a mustard seed that someone took and sowed in the garden; it grew and became a tree, and the birds of the air made nests in its branches." And again he said, "To what should I compare the kingdom of God? It is like yeast that a woman took and mixed in with three measures of flour until all of it was leavened."

Lk 13:18–21

"What is the kingdom of God like?"

The two parables of the kingdom of God—the parables of the tiny mustard seed and the yeast—are not simply nice images meant to evoke imagination. Parables are explosive accounts of what is most true. The kingdom of God will take root, as a tree, and transfigure this world. Like yeast, it will penetrate governments, education, philosophy, financial enterprises, families, and human hearts. The daily news convinces us this is not happening. Jesus promises us it is. When? The coming of the kingdom does not happen on our timetable, but on God's. Until the kingdom of God has become the kingdom of this world, Christians offer the world a visual parable of the kingdom of God. Those who do not yet believe must be able to see in our personal, family, and professional lives an answer to the question, "What is the kingdom of God like?"

How much trust you have in me, Jesus. You are trusting that my life will visually demonstrate the values and gifts of your kingdom. I am nothing without you. Shape my mind, will, and heart to be a sign of your love.

95 *Running the race*

As for me, I am already being poured out as a libation, and the time of my departure has come. I have fought the good fight, I have finished the race, I have kept the faith. From now on there is reserved for me the crown of righteousness, which the Lord, the righteous judge, will give me on that day, and not only to me but also to all who have longed for his appearing.

2 Tim 4:6–8

" . . . I have finished the race. . . ."

Paul the Apostle. Teresa of Avila. John of the Cross. Francis of Assisi. Elizabeth Ann Seton. John Paul II. Mother Teresa. These individuals not only ran the race, they believed that this race was the only race worth running: the race laid out by the life, death, and resurrection of Christ Jesus. It is marked by his life, and culminates in the mystery of his—and our—death and resurrection.

On the way we are accompanied by the Spirit and fed by the Lord's Body in the Eucharist.

I was just reading a magazine as I waited in a doctor's office. A Christian musician was grieving at the death of his child, and in his pain still believed. A politician's wife forgave her husband's affair in order to keep the family together. A lieutenant colonel started a scholarship fund for the children of soldiers killed in Iraq. They too are running the race. Who do *you* know who is racing on the way of Christ Jesus? How can you support them? Urge them on? Applaud them?

What a parade, dear Lord, is yours. Your people are everywhere in the world surprising everyone with their generosity, forgiveness, valor, and selfless charity. Help me to strengthen them, to cheer them on their way.

96 Beautiful lives

Again he entered the synagogue, and a man was there who had a withered hand. They watched him to see whether he would cure him on the sabbath, so that they might accuse him. And he said to the man who had the withered hand, "Come forward." Then he said to them, "Is it lawful to do good or to do harm on the sabbath, to save life or to kill?" But they were silent. He looked around at them with anger; he was grieved at their hardness of heart and said to the man, "Stretch out your hand." He stretched it out, and his hand was restored. The Pharisees went out and immediately conspired with the Herodians against him, how to destroy him.

Mk 3:1–6

" . . . [Jesus] was grieved at their hardness of heart. . . ."

This Gospel reading is about broken hearts. Jesus was grieved, saddened, heartbroken at the Pharisees' hardness of heart. The saints truly know what this means. They know that when we shut God out of our lives, not only are *our* hearts broken, but so also is *God's*. The saints thirsted for the opportunity to be with God in the same way a person in love desires to please their loved one. Whatever their age or vocation—mothers or fathers, kings or queens, religious, priests, or popes, doctors, children or young adults—every aspect of their day was lifted up in the experience of Jesus gazing on them, calling them, loving them, and even wanting to love others through them. The beauty of their lives attracted others because they gave God their voice to speak his words, their hands and feet in service, their eyes that those who met them could feel that God himself cared about them. On the physical level, clogged arteries can lead to heart attacks and death. Let us unblock our spiritual arteries. Let us arouse our love, stoke the fires of devotion, read the word of God, and receive God's grace in the sacraments to keep our hearts soft and open to receive the gift of God.

Lord, set my heart on fire!

97 *Living on a larger stage*

The LORD is my light and my salvation;
     whom shall I fear?
. . . Though an army encamp against me,
     my heart shall not fear;
though war rise up against me,
     yet I will be confident.
Hear, O LORD, when I cry aloud,
     be gracious to me and answer me!
"Come," my heart says, "seek his face!"
. . . Do not give me up to the will of my adversaries,
     for false witnesses have risen against me,
     and they are breathing out violence.
I believe that I shall see the goodness of the LORD. . . .

Ps 27:1, 3, 7–8, 12–13

". . . yet I will be confident."

The psalmist wrote this prayer in what seems to be a situation of grave threat to his life. The imagery he uses to describe his fear heightens in intensity: first he speaks of fear; then he speaks of an army encircling him;

finally he uses the imagery of all-out war. The cause of his anguish is clarified in verse twelve: he has been falsely accused, which at that time could lead to death. In the midst of this harrowing situation that must have filled him with mortal anguish, the psalmist still proclaims his belief that he shall see the goodness of the Lord. This psalm makes me think of Susanna in the Old Testament, of John the Baptist, Jesus, Peter, and Paul, of contemporary figures such as Anne Frank, Etty Hillesum, and Nelson Mandela. These individuals realized that the drama of their life was played out on a larger stage than their suffering alone. They discovered that they could bear everything and grow stronger through it, and that to live full of fear, anguish, bitterness, and hatred is truly to be deprived of life. They experienced that the loss of all one treasures in life, even the loss of one's life itself, has a deeper meaning. We must listen to our hearts, seek the Lord's face, and wait for him to act.

My soul, give praise to the Lord. All the days I live may I bless his holy name.

98 *Build others up*

Blessed are the meek, for they will inherit the earth. . . .

Jesus called them to him and said, "You know that the rulers of the Gentiles lord it over them, and their great ones are tyrants over them. It will not be so among you; but whoever wishes to be great among you must be your servant, and whoever wishes to be first among you must be your slave; just as the Son of Man came not to be served but to serve, and to give his life a ransom for many."

Mt 5:5; 20:25–28

"It will not be so among you. . . ."

Meek people are undemanding. Jesus is not speaking here of those who are naturally meek-tempered, nor is he speaking of the weak-willed. Jesus is referring to people who are not controlled by their unconscious needs for power, control, security, affection, comfort, and esteem. When an event triggers their hidden agendas, they have learned to step back and seize the opportunity to break the cycle of anger and frustration. How? We all are triggered by people and events, and if we aren't careful, the way we react betrays that we are indeed "full of ourselves." Meek people have learned to let go and empty themselves of their addictive needs. They have discovered that they are much more than a good name, a new car, the latest gadget, a promotion, a relationship. They have learned to see themselves from the perspective of God's watchful presence. Just as God builds them up, so they become persons who return good for evil with a view to build others up, to re-create a situation or person or relationship. They become meek because they are emptied of self-conceit.

Catch me, Lord, when I am becoming too full of myself. Catch me by surprise and attract me to the beauty of a meek life.

99 *See with the eyes of the heart*

When the Son of Man comes in his glory . . . he will sit upon his glorious throne, and all the nations will be assembled before him. . . . Then the king will say to those on his right, "Come, you who are blessed by my Father. Inherit the kingdom prepared for you from the foundation of the world. For I was hungry and you gave me food, I was thirsty and you gave me drink, a stranger and you welcomed me, naked and you clothed me, ill and you cared for me, in prison and you visited me." . . . And the king will say to them in reply, "Amen, I say to you, whatever you did for one of these least brothers of mine, you did for me."

Mt 25:31–32, 34–36, 40 (NABRE)

"Whatever you did for one of these least brothers of mine, you did for me."

Our society has an insatiable need for unlimited economic growth. This creates both material and spiritual underdevelopment throughout the world, giving rise to a shameful poverty and human indignity. It is time for us to remember that the relationship between humanity and the living God is the true inner structure and authentic meaning of the world. The human person is a child of God, brought into existence by God's creative word and immense love. Each of us, and all of us together, share the world's resources for the period of time that is our life. It is the prayer of the rich and the prayer of the poor, the love of the rich and the love of the poor that break open the seemingly impossible impasse the world is in: the poor you will always have with you (cf. Mt 26:11). It is people who can see with the eyes of the heart, people, whether rich or poor, who can love together. It is these people who become the secret makers of a new history and who hasten the coming of the kingdom of God.

May I join hands and hearts with all the people I encounter. May I think about them with compassion, speak to them in gentleness, and shoulder with them the responsibility of shaping a new way for humanity.

100 *It's all about love*

When they had finished breakfast, Jesus said to Simon Peter, "Simon son of John, do you love me more than these?" He said to him, "Yes, Lord; you know that I love you." Jesus said to him, "Feed my lambs." A second time he said to him, "Simon son of John, do you love me?" He said to him, "Yes, Lord; you know that I love you." Jesus said to him, "Tend my sheep." He said to him the third time, "Simon son of John, do you love me?" . . . And he said to him, "Lord, you know everything; you know that I love you." Jesus said to him, "Feed my sheep. . . ." After this he said to him, "Follow me."

Jn 21:15–17, 19

" . . . do you love me . . . Follow me."

Peter. We hear his first recorded words in the Gospel, "Go away from me, Lord, for I am a sinful man!" (Lk 5:8–10), to which Jesus responds, *Follow me*. We watch the apostle later try to convince his Master not to go to his passion and death. To which Jesus retorts, *Get behind me. You are not thinking as God thinks.* We are a bit taken aback when Peter states that he would die for Jesus, only to hear that he would instead, that very night, deny he ever knew his Lord. Now finally, we hear these last precious words between Peter and Jesus preserved in this Gospel passage. This time, however, it is the Lord who begins the conversation. *Peter, do you love me?* Thrice he asks the brave apostle who pledged his very life for Jesus this simple question that cuts to the quick: "Do you love me?" So this is what it is all about. *Love.* No great drama or accomplishments or heroism. It is all about answering this longing of Jesus to be loved. That's all. And if we do love him, then we will hear with new ears the invitation offered again and again: *If you love me, follow me.*

Yes, Lord, I love you. But I know I also am, like Peter, "a sinful man." Will you accept this humble offer of my heart?

Indexes

Liturgical Index

(Numbers refer to chapter numbers.)

Topical Index

(Numbers refer to chapter numbers.)

ANGER

ANXIETY

CONVERSION

Discipleship

Fear

Frustration

Joy

Scriptural Index

(Numbers in bold refer to chapter numbers.)

KATHRYN JAMES HERMES, a member of the Daughters of St. Paul since 1978, holds an M.T.S. from Weston Jesuit School of Theology and an advanced certificate in Scripture. Besides her work for Pauline Books & Media e-media development,  Sister Kathryn is a frequent contributor to *Living Faith* magazine, and gives numerous presentations throughout the country. Her published books are available in print and e-book format:

Surviving Depression

Holding on to Hope

Making Peace with Yourself

Beginning Contemplative Prayer

Minute Meditations for Lent

St. Joseph: Help for Life's Emergencies

Jesus: Help in Every Need

A Simple Life: Wisdom from Jane de Chantal

Inner Peace: Wisdom from Jean-Pierre de Caussade